Thank you
being you.

It is an absolute
honor and privilege
to serve.

Embrace what is
with trust and
calmness for clarity
to emerge to live
a life in FLOW....

Love,
Feisal

four steps to
FLOW

the art of living a meaningful life
head and heart united

feisal alibhai

Qineticare Ltd.
Unit 2402, Tower II, Admiralty Centre,
No. 18 Harcourt Road, Hong Kong
www.qineticare.com

First Qineticare Ltd. Edition December 2018.

For more information about special discounts for bulk
purchases, or request for feisal alibhai to speak at your
event, please contact Qineticare at +852 3693 7520
or email enquiries@qineticare.com

ISBN: 978-988-79460-2-1

To mummy and papa for your unconditional love
and
Mahdi and Kazim for the privilege of being your baba

Contents

Acknowledgments

Dr. Kevin Loh my oncologist for being a godsend with hands of healing power. Your love and care for me and all of those we have served together is beyond words.

Dr. John Simon my internist for always being there through my various unexpected adventures and for your tenaciousness in getting to the bottom of what many specialists couldn't, while we both served others.

To Anisa my kinesiologist, who was the first to burst my ego bubble and help me become real.

Dr. Dwarakanath and Andrea for helping me to become the sun in my solar system.

Thank you Robin Sharma for pushing me to ask myself the five things that need to happen between now and when it's time. Qineticare is the result of this.

Dr. Shefali Tsabary for the deep caring and loving energy you showered on me and my family.

Dr. Habib Sadeghi, for creating a safe space to have the conversations that needed to happen without expectation, imposition, or judgment.

Tony Robbins, for creating such a gut-wrenching experience that enabled me to move toward being my true self when

I had bottomed out.

To Uzma for your presence through one of the most challenging experiences of my life and being such a great teacher.

To Faris for dropping everything to be with me as I came within an inch of my life.

Mehmood for being a pillar of strength through thick and thin with unwavering love and care.

Shayda, you have been more than the sister I never had. I am so grateful for you being in my life.

Adnan, you have been a rock with a soft and caring center.

Jason, Carlos, and Alain for being my true brothers from another mother.

Danette, I am so blessed by your unwavering love and support.

Yatish, you have been a dear friend and guide.

To my stubborn Yorkshireman editor David Robert Ord, without whom the flow of this book would not have been possible.

My beloved Suz, you taught me how to open my heart and love again.

Foreword

When Feisal shared the incredible journey he has taken, especially during the past dozen or more years, I recognized that this was one of those rare adventures others need to hear about in order to inspire them to uncover within themselves potential they presently have no clue exists.

It had never occurred to Feisal that he should write a book. A businessman with an amazing track record at a young age, living in the exciting metropolis of Hong Kong, he connected with me during one of his many trips to the United States because, with his two sons now in their teens, he wanted to be certain that his approach to the challenges and quandaries a parent faces with boys of this age was thoroughly grounded in the most conscious approach to parenting.

When challenged by something, he researches and researches, traveling the world not only for his business pursuits but to further his understanding of what's required to live an exceptional life. I connected with him at a point in his journey where he had increasingly come to understand the importance of using both head and heart to decipher the optimum course in each and every situation, charting from deep within himself the path of greatest authenticity and wisdom.

It's rare for a business tycoon with the kind of success Feisal enjoyed to approach every aspect of life from such a highly aware state. I suggested a book and put him in touch with my editor. The result is the amazing journey, laced with abundant flashes of insight and a wealth of inspiration, you now hold in your hands.

I know what it's like to go through a transformation that completely alters and elevates your awareness. When I wrote my first book The Conscious Parent, to be followed by Out of Control and The Awakened Family, I laid out a strategy for parenting that flew in the face of pretty much everything the popular culture and even most parenting experts advocate when it comes to how to raise children. What I shared, and that Oprah so graciously picked up on and trumpeted to the world, came to me as a result of questioning everything I had ever believed.

Feisal's metamorphosis in the world of business took a very different course, and yet led to a parallel eye-opening experience. As happened in my own case, he experienced a coming together of head and heart.

There's a widespread move today to denigrate the mind. People are encouraged to get out of their head and into their heart. It can sound so persuasive. But as Feisal amply demonstrates from his own experience, it doesn't work. We need to use our head as well as our heart. It isn't a case of one or the other, since the two aren't opposites but two faces of a single reality.

When we are attuned to both head and heart, we experience a centeredness, a calmness, a peace. We are simultaneously alive to the wisest of insights and the deepest of feelings, which when accessed in the way Feisal describes allows for a truly holistic experience.

If you were to meet Feisal, you would be amazed by his undaunted spirit, his seemingly inexhaustible energy, and his boundless enthusiasm. Most of all, you would experience a level of attention to detail and a deep caring that's truly a rare find.

It's my hope that these aspects of this quite unique individual will inspire you to discover within yourself some of what Feisal exudes on a daily basis with everyone he encounters. As you read these life-changing words, allow the insight that made him the person he is today to uplift you, raising your consciousness and transforming you.

Dr. Shefali Tsabary, New York, NY
Author: *The Conscious Parent*
Out of Control
The Awakened Family

Preface

Author M. Scott Peck begins his landmark book *The Road Less Traveled* with the simple but powerful observation, "Life is difficult." I would add that life is a singular journey. Although we may share certain universal experiences, how we find ourselves in specific circumstances, especially the painful ones, is the result of forging a path made of choices that are uniquely our own. While family and friends can be of great help during difficult times, ultimately we bear our burdens alone. Only we can make each new decision for ourselves and in the process, taking personal responsibility for the outcome no matter where the road leads.

When I first met Feisal, he was exactly what I expected him to be—organized, ambitious, confident, and powerfully connected. He was the ideal image of the 21st century international entrepreneur of a multimillion-dollar company. Replete with material success, his life was one most people could only dream of living. Then suddenly everything was turned upside down when he found himself facing a serious health crisis and blindsided by divorce, virtually at the same time. I can still recall his desperation as he tried to understand why these things had happened to him and struggled with the fact that for the first time in his life, his power, connections, intellect, and even wealth were of little use in finding resolution or lasting peace.

As a self-made man, Feisal isn't one to wait for things to happen. His success is a direct result of being a lifelong student of self-improvement and always applying new principles to his life with great effect. For years his life involved an endless stream of books, workshops, retreats, motivational seminars, and coaching sessions, all of them designed to help him meet greater challenges and accomplish more. When crisis strikes however, finding peace and healing can be elusive for such a driven type-A personality. I know because I am one. We're doers. We take action. We're about devising a plan and executing it to reach a predetermined goal—mission accomplished and on to the next challenge.

While this approach might work well for business, it's completely ineffective for resolving the personal challenges of life. I figured this out during my own crisis with cancer over 20 years ago, when I took a year's sabbatical from medical school to reassess my priorities, ask myself some really difficult questions, and search my heart and mind for the answers I needed. The result of this yearlong journey of introspection and emotional resolution was a healing process I created and published called *The Clarity Cleanse*, a protocol for realizing and releasing unresolved emotional issues so that the physical body is freer to heal in the absence of both conscious and unconscious negative energy.

For Feisal to begin his healing journey, I insisted he discontinue all self-improvement and consider the fact that he alone was enough to heal his life and body exactly as he was. The answers weren't outside himself in a book, life coach, or anywhere else. They were inside him at a deeper level of consciousness, and it was our job to work together to uncover them.

When life is a constant drive to become the best at everything, it can be unnerving to simply stop and realize how little is actually under our direct control. Getting off the treadmill and resisting the urge to fix everything right now can seem like we are doing nothing. For a driven person, it can feel counterintuitive or even irresponsible. But getting rid of all the distractions of life and the mental noise that comes along with them is the first essential step in creating the space in one's life, mind, and heart for the answers to enter. It's in that space, that opening, where clarity occurs regarding why certain things are happening, the role personal responsibility plays in those events, and what needs to be done to resolve or reconcile the situation.

The mind and body are inextricably connected. After more than 20 years of seeing patients heal emotionally, then watching their bodies respond physically, I can attest that healing is as much about what we don't do as it is about what we choose to do. With this in mind, Feisal stopped searching for the answers outside of himself and embarked on one of the bravest healing journeys I've had the privilege to witness.

Because we are the only ones making choices for ourselves, wherever those choices lead us and the outcomes they produce are solely of our own making. This is one of the primary tenets of achieving clarity. Ultimately each of us must take 100% personal responsibility for the present condition of our lives. If we don't, we remain stuck in our circumstances until someone else does something we want or changes in a way we prefer.

To give other people or things such power over our happiness is to live an impotent, disempowered life. It's to give others control over us and make ourselves their prisoner. By taking full responsibility for every choice that led up to the conditions we find our lives in today, we get 100% of the power to change our circumstances. The first step toward living an authentic life is owning it—all of it. Feisal does that with a courage and conviction I've rarely seen.

It's hard to let go and trust that the healing process is leading us in the direction that's most beneficial for us, which is most often away from what we think we want and toward what we need. It's clarity that helps us understand this essential difference. Clarity also opens a space in our heart for love to enter. Love is the greatest healing power in existence. When we apply love to the places inside ourselves that are hurting—by exercising compassion, understanding and self-forgiveness—we interact with the world in a more loving way. Our circumstances begin to change because we have changed. Of course, it takes great courage and vulnerability to love, especially ourselves, but there is hardly anything we mistakenly search for more in the outside world than love. The great Persian poet Rumi said that our job isn't to look for love, but to remove all the barriers we have to the love that already exists for us.

I sat with Feisal and his beloved ex-wife, Uzma, working through a couple's intervention we call S.oul-ution i.ntegration T.rio (S.i.T.), and ultimately the process of Conscious Completion of their marriage energetically. What impressed me most was the realization by both of them that while this may have been the end of their marriage, it wasn't the end of their lives together, as there were many more moments to be shared and memories to be made between them and their children for years to come. They had fulfilled the higher purpose they were destined to provide each other with as husband and wife and were now taking those lessons into a new, deeper, and richer phase of their lives together.

Naturally this requires a higher level of consciousness and living in a new line of energy that only clarity can provide. It also gives one the power to reframe experiences by recognizing the hidden gift that comes wrapped in each of our problems and allows us to choose how we experience each situation. As I tell all my patients with regard to healing, it's not the issue at hand that's most important, but how we relate to it.

Discovering why our lives are the way they are can be quite an epiphany. With the right amount of honesty and hard work, a person is rarely the same after such an experience. This is often why people state that their biggest tragedy turned out to be the biggest blessing, because the painful circumstances brought about changes in them and their lives that couldn't have happened any other way. I know it's certainly true for both myself and Feisal.

Rarely have I seen a person so courageously dedicated to his own healing. It's my hope that readers are as inspired by reading about his journey as I was in witnessing it. His victory over what can only be described as a true "dark night of the soul" confirms that he is a genuine success not only in the ways of the world, but also in the ways of the heart.

Dr. Habib Sadeghi
Agoura Hills, CA
Author: *The Clarity Cleanse*
www.BeHiveofHealing.com

1

The Challenge of Opportunity

It's said that there's nothing surer than death and taxes. What isn't widely acknowledged is that there's a close runner up, and that's the certainty of *change*.

No aspect of life is immune to change, whether we are talking about our financial affairs, our health, or our relationships with others. Change is a reality none of us can escape and constitutes one of our greatest challenges.

When things don't go the way we hoped they would and change is forced on us, the question becomes, *How am I going to cope?*

Each of us has to answer for ourselves, Am I going to resist the change, or succumb to it and allow it to make me miserable—or might there be a more beneficial response?

Particularly if a change affects one of the key areas of life, our tendency is to react, which often involves considerable anger. If this doesn't get us anywhere, we may descend into despondency as we simply resign ourselves to what's happening.

When a business investment fails, a serious health issue arises, or our significant other leaves us, the last thing we're likely to conclude is that *what's happening is for our benefit.*

Life has shown me that although it may not look like it, any serious change short of losing our life is an invitation to convert the challenge we are faced with into *opportunity.*

This may surprise you, but I've also come to see that the more egregious an apparent setback to our hopes and dreams, *the more likely it is to have the potential to be the making of us.*

To illustrate what I'm saying, it so happens that I'm writing not long after the renowned Cambridge theoretical physicist Stephen Hawking's death. By living to age 76, he beat the prognosis that emerged from his diagnosis by over half a century. Diagnosed when he was only 21, he wasn't expected to see his 25th birthday.

Hawking's illness gave him a new zest for life. Describing himself as "bored" before he became ill, he said of his affliction that "although there was a cloud hanging over my future, I found, to my surprise, that I was enjoying life in the present more than before."

To be hit in the stomach certainly doesn't inspire us to embrace what's happening to us, let alone to trust that life is on our side. Yet I'm going to suggest that at every turn, life constantly asks of us a willingness to *embrace what's happening, no matter how things may appear.*

To embrace life when everything seems to be going wrong is counterintuitive—especially in the face of a catastrophic failure of our business, our health, or a relationship to which we have made a significant commitment. We are asked to be at peace with ourselves, at peace with what's happening, and at peace with those around us...at a time when the last thing we're likely to be feeling is any sort of peacefulness.

We are talking about embracing not only difficulties, but real turning-points—including the kind of crises that are life-threatening, such as a serious accident or cancer.

Instead of either capitulating to his affliction and becoming despondent, or feeling angry at life because of the illness that had befallen him, Stephen Hawking embraced what was happening in the certainty that his presence on the planet could yet serve a purpose. Choosing to regard being confined to a wheelchair as an opportunity, he plunged deep into the world of astrophysics.

When we embrace change instead of pushing back, something amazing happens. We find ourselves moving into a state of trust, whereby we spontaneously *move forward confidently*.

When life as we dream it ought to be falls apart, most of us tell ourselves, "This shouldn't be happening. This isn't what I signed up for." In contrast, when we come from a place of trust as Hawking did, we take a different approach.

Whether it's your team at work, your family at home, or members of an organization to which you belong, you can help them deal with change by training yourself to embrace the situation as an opportunity, then trusting your ability to harness it for your further development as a person. It's about "keeping calm and carrying on" as Queen Elizabeth II is famous for advocating. When this is your response, you clear the way for the optimal course of action to arise spontaneously from *within* you.

To trust like this involves recovering the modus operandi with which we functioned when we were young. Back then, we didn't engage in endlessly second-guessing ourselves, and neither were we besieged by doubt. After the initial shock that accompanied a challenge, we quickly settled ourselves down, finding within ourselves the resilience to move forward trustingly. Within minutes of a fall in which we bashed a knee, or following a squabble with another child in the sandpit over a toy, we were soon playing happily again.

This childhood ability to have our initial tendency to get upset morph into trust, so that our anxiety subsides and we return to a state of calmness, still resides within us. No matter our age, at any moment we can awaken afresh to the realization that many occurrences that initially appear threatening are actually the universe beckoning us to adventure. After the shock of our changed circumstances, if we wisely choose to allow our thoughts to quiet down, a peacefulness quite naturally washes over us.

Let me illustrate what this looks like in real terms of my personal experience with my health. At the age of 35, at the pinnacle of my success, I was stricken with a life-threatening illness. My diagnosis came as a complete shock. I was about to have dinner the evening before I was due to leave for my annual vacation. As I took the first bite, I found myself choking. Following the vacation, during which I inexplicably lost five kilos despite eating well, I spent the following week in Hong Kong undergoing an endoscopy, a colonoscopy, and a CT of my neck. I was told I had reflux and a hematoma, both of which were eminently manageable.

The next three weeks were spent in Mozambique, Angola, and the Democratic Republic of Congo working with the various multinationals who were visiting to continue growing our highly successful fast-moving consumer goods distribution business. I then continued on to Dubai and Pakistan, where we were looking at establishing truck and motorcycle assembly plants.

As a result of the tests I had undergone in Hong Kong, I was taking medication for the choking. Now other symptoms began appearing. Since I was a person who regularly worked 15 or 16 hours straight without tiring, the people with me were shocked to see my energy plummet. Ascending a flight of stairs in Angola, I felt as if I had asthma. Then in Pakistan, on my way to and back from the site where we wanted to put the factory, I fell asleep, which surprised everybody.

Upon returning to Hong Kong, more tests were ordered. Had the doctors missed something? The focus was on the possibility that, due to my frequent travel to exotic countries, I had contracted a tropical disease. But despite extensive testing, nothing showed up.

I told my doctor, "Pretend you don't know me from Adam. Start from the basics with a clean slate." We began with blood work, an x-ray, and various other tests.

I was sitting in front of my doctor when the nurse entered unexpectedly with the x-ray. When he examined it, his face turned white. Leaning over to peer at the image, I asked, "Where's my lung, doc?"

My lung had collapsed and one side of the x-ray was dark. On my way out the door, the doctor urged, "Whatever God you believe in, please pray." Since doctors don't normally talk about God until it's the beginning of the end, I was beyond shocked.

The following day I was again in the doctor's office awaiting the verbal results of a PET/CT scan taken during the morning. "I'm sorry, but I have bad news," he announced, "you have cancer."

It turned out I had stage three cancer consisting of ten tumors. The largest, the size of a Rubik's cube, was in the center of my chest, which accounted for my breathing problem and why swallowing was difficult. In my neck was a tumor the equivalent of a tennis ball in size. A further eight tumors populated my lungs.

At the time of my diagnosis, my company was operating in seven countries in war-torn Africa and five in Eastern Europe, as well as maintaining buying offices in Dubai, Paris, and Hong Kong. I had thousands of employees for whom I was responsible. I knew instantly what I needed to do. The company had to be handed over to my partners for the duration of my treatment. This was a matter of my personal survival and required a complete cessation of work and a total focus on recovery.

The handover took no more than five minutes and was executed in my hospital room two days after my diagnosis. I informed the team, "I travel six months of the year and thus don't run the business day-to-day. The one-year plan is done and so is the five-year. I am no longer active CEO and want you to pretend I'm on extended leave. At risk of being fired, I'm to be given no reports of any kind by anyone."

I initially identified four critical elements if I was to have any hope of recovery. These involved access to the best medical care, either medical insurance or the financial means to afford the best care, family support, and a purpose for living. Fortunately I had all of these—especially the will to live, as my sons were only one and three.

I spent the next eleven months between home and hospital, undergoing twenty rounds of chemo and three surgeries. There were moments when I came within an inch of death. The treatment was an extremely painful and frightening ordeal.

When my remission was in due course confirmed, I was given a 50-50 chance of a recurrence—not odds I cared to hear. However, during the eleven months of treatment, I had researched extensively how I might have unwittingly contributed to my illness, and consequently was increasingly aware of the many ways in which I had lived a life of imbalance. This insight enabled me to determine a plan of action, both for my recovery and in order to live a full life after returning to work.

As I came to see how my imbalance had adversely impacted not only my physical health but also the wellbeing of my family, my spirituality, and at times even my incredibly successful career, I sought to live more healthily. To achieve this, I assembled a team of experts in various fields whose focus was on holistic practices that could aid my recovery.

By now I was acutely aware that in addition to the finest medical treatment, to learn and live a balanced life was the key to not only my survival but my life going forward. The holistic approach I had begun practicing during my near-death crisis taught me we must never approach life in a compartmentalized way or we will pay a price. As a result of spending my days in this quite different manner, it's now been thirteen years since I entered remission.

Stewing emotions and racing thoughts will torpedo the trust you need in a time of crisis in order to proceed in the most advantageous manner instead of being filled with anxiety and acting from a state of panic. Yet isn't this how most of us react? The clarity we require if we are to make wise choices at critical moments results from approaching such challenges in a trusting manner, instead of with our thoughts running wild and our emotions in turmoil.

Instead of scrambling to know what to do next, the stillness that arises within us when we choose to embrace change allows us to hear ourselves *think* in a way we haven't until now. Along with the clarity of mind that comes to us, we also find ourselves aware of what we truly *feel* about things, which may be quite different from what we've been told all our life we're supposed to feel.

The quieting of our racing thoughts, when coupled with emotional calmness, allows the kind of insight to emerge that unites the wisdom of both head *and* heart. As head and heart come together, we find ourselves shifting from *chaos to clarity.*

This synergy of mental awareness and deep feeling enables us to move forward in what's commonly referred to as "flow." Science writer Daniel Goleman, who became famed for his coverage of the behavioral and brain sciences in his *New York Times* columns, says in his book *Emotional Intelligence* that measurements of brainwaves show that the state of flow is one in which the brain quiets down. There's a lessening of cortical arousal, which he describes as a cool state that's devoid of our usual emotional static.

When we embrace change instead of either resisting or ranting, we enter into a trusting frame of mind in which the clarity that arises promotes the kind of action characterized by flow. The ability to keep a cool head no matter what empowers us to turn challenge into opportunity.

I have described a watershed experience that allowed me to shift into a life marked by flow. As a result of *three* watershed crises life put me through, the other two of which I will describe in due course, today I experience myself being carried forward by a powerful current in more and more areas of my life. This calm current emanates from the essence of who I find myself to be, as expressed through both head and heart.

The insight, wisdom, creativity, and energy I enjoy mirror the state athletes and creative individuals refer to when they speak of being "in the zone." Those who regularly experience the zone describe it as a mode of being in which excellence becomes effortless. Whether in athletics, the arts, or our business life, everything peripheral disappears in a blissful, steady absorption in the moment.

Despite earlier injury that had taken her out of the sport following her first gold medal, American Alpine ski racer Diane Roffe-Steinrotter captured a second gold in the 1994 Winter Olympics. Asked about her experience as she raced for that second gold, she remarked that she remembered nothing about it other than—you'll hardly believe the expression she used—"being immersed in *relaxation*."

When we're in flow, we accomplish a tremendous amount, but it isn't at all stressful. Although fully engaged, we're relaxed. As you'll hear in the chapters ahead, I'm well acquainted with stress and the catastrophic consequences it can reap. It's what taught me how to be even more productive while in a relaxed state of flow than when I was driven.

Post-impressionist painter Paul Cezanne described flow as an artist. "Right now a moment of time is fleeting by! Capture its reality in paint! To do that we must put all else out of our minds. We must become that moment, make ourselves a sensitive recording plate…give the image of what we actually see, forgetting everything that has been seen before our time."

Because flow is a heightened state of awareness, it enables us to learn from the past without constantly rehashing it and indulging in "if only." It enables us to plan for the future without becoming entangled in "what if." Yesterday and tomorrow don't intrude upon the experience of today.

You can't be bored, can't be depressed, can't be at all anxious and be in a state of flow, because when you're in flow you aren't dwelling on yourself and your problems. In flow it's as if you forget about yourself. Your mind is wonderfully alert, but in a different way from the unproductive mental chatter we engage in so much of the time.

Goleman says that in flow our emotions are contained and channeled, so that they are aligned with the task at hand. We're absorbed in what we're doing to the point our awareness is merged with our actions. We're completely present in whatever we may be doing, our attention undivided. In this state of presence, we enjoy a crystal clear awareness of the path that's right for us in any given situation. As I have described, this is also a powerful aid to enjoying a state of health and wellbeing.

Let me be clear what I have in mind when I speak of "presence." It's become popular to refer to presence as a state of "being," which many then contrast with what they think of as "doing." It's as if being is the opposite of taking action. To imagine being and doing contradict one another isn't only to fail to grasp what it means to be "present," it's to lack comprehension of what embracing a situation involves, as well as to fail to understand the state of flow.

I constantly hear people pitting being against doing, claiming that if we resolutely "affirm" that something will happen, it will happen. This becomes an excuse to hope for something better while using the idea of "being" as an excuse *not to do anything to bring it about.*

Being and doing are two sides of a single coin. If there's to be change, from being must come doing. This is the case whether an issue is of a personal nature, interpersonal, or global. Being is the way we get clear about what needs to happen. Once we are clear, we move into a state of flow from which we start making things happen. It's important to understand how being and doing are synergistic, since it's the synergy that empowers us to be in the state of presence and therefore in flow.

Presence isn't to be equated with doing nothing. Equally, flow has nothing in common with floating idly downstream subject to life's whims. Quite the opposite, flow is when head and heart unite in dynamic action that's free of all pressure— free of the drivenness that, as you'll shortly see, almost put me in my grave.

A composer described those moments when his work is at its best. "You yourself are in an ecstatic state to such a point that you feel as though you almost don't exist." He added that not only are you in wonderment, the creativity just flows out of you. This is the state depicted in the words of the Tao Te Ching when it advises, "Act without doing, work without effort."

While on the one hand things become practically effortless when we are in flow, on the other hand our whole being shifts into the sort of "immersed" state Olympic skier Diane Roffe-Steinrotter described. We become keenly aware, agile in mind, deeply feeling, and ready to move at a moment's notice in whatever direction our intuition asks of us.

Chuang Tzu, the Chinese mystic-philosopher and fellow Taoist of Lao Tzu, described one who lives in the present as one who "plays in the one breath of heaven and earth." Breath here is the Chinese word *qi*, or in English *chi,* which denotes the life-giving force, the spirit, that gives being to every person, thing, and event in the universe. The life of a person who experiences this total sense of being is carried along by the power and purpose of this force, so that whatever she or he may be engaged in, they are literally "playing" as they once did as a child.

Previously when I planned trips associated with my businesses, I've had people say to me, "What an intense schedule." My response is that because it's something I really want to do, or if I'm doing it with someone I care about, I never find it intense. I'm actually amazed how effortless such a schedule can feel. Whenever I work, which involves much travel, to me it's play.

If you're doing something that doesn't really interest you, I can see how it can be arduous. I believe in the kind of "work" that doesn't feel like work but is simply an expression of my creativity, so that it's an outpouring of who I find myself to be. I simply show up and do what I need to do. Because I'm immersed in it, it never occurs to me to think to myself, "This is so tough."

Although playing comes naturally to a child, as we grow up anxieties crowd in upon us and we lose the ability to be absorbed in the simplest of things in the way we once were.

Consequently we have to go through growing up all over again, this time emotionally as we learn to rein in our reactions and silence our mind chatter.

Flow is the state Jesus was pointing to when he said, "Out of your innermost being will *flow rivers of living water*." Do you know how Diane described the state she was in as she raced for her second gold? "I felt like a *waterfall*," she said.

Perhaps you've experienced flow at some time or other. It's exhilarating when it happens, isn't it? Well, I propose that these peak moments open a window onto the possibility of living the whole of life in such a state.

The Buddha came to understand this, pointing us toward not just how we can experience times of flow, but a *lifetime* of flow. To have a Buddha mind is to be in flow.

On the 80th birthday of acclaimed Italian conductor Arturo Toscanini, someone asked his son Walter what his father ranked as his most important achievement. The son replied, "For him there can be no such thing. Whatever he happens to be doing at the moment is the biggest thing in his life—whether it is conducting a symphony or peeling an orange."

As I invite you to journey with me into a life in which change becomes opportunity and challenge is seen as adventure, I ask you to ponder the wise words of Joseph Campbell: "People say that what we're all seeking is a meaning for life. I think that what we're really seeking is an experience of being alive, so that our life experiences on the purely physical plane will have resonance within our innermost being and reality, so that we can actually feel the rapture of being alive."

2

"*Am I Good Enough?*"

To embrace a situation trustingly and flow with it is fundamentally different from how most of us conduct our lives.

Picture flow as a centered life in which there's complete balance. To either side of this centered state lies one of two unbalanced modes of making our way in the world.

One of these modes involves needing to prove ourselves. When we operate in this mode, we are in a state of resistance to whatever may be happening. We fight everything that gets in the way of how we imagine things should be.

The other mode is one in which we tend to capitulate to our circumstances. Many believe they shouldn't oppose what may be happening in their life because something is either meant to be or not meant to be. People speak of something being their fate. They talk about it being in their stars or not in their cards. Accepting whatever comes their way is seen as submitting to the "will of God."

Whether you are inclined to be driven as I was, or to allow life to toss you around as you tell yourself somthing is or isn't meant to be, one question tends to haunt us all. That question is, *Am I good enough?*

Because I exuded self-confidence, no one imagined I harbored my share of self-doubt. But like everyone else on the planet, I too struggled with a need to prove I was good enough—an issue that I'm now convinced lies at the heart of the human predicament.

In different degrees, all of us are faced with the question of *whether we are good enough.*

Despite the fact I was proficient in my business, as well as having come from a solidly reputable and successful family, pretty much everything I did in my life up until age 35 was laced with insecurity.

Since the fact I was born to be a dealmaker was clear not only to myself but to everyone who knew me, and I was naturally good at it, why would I be insecure? Why did I feel a need to prove myself? With what I had accomplished by such a young age, you'd think I wouldn't have even a smidgeon of self-doubt.

In the minds of the public, self-doubt is associated with those on the lower rungs of the social ladder, not with the world's super-successful—the rich and famous, the stars and trendsetters. In reality self-doubt is why even some of the most talented people on the planet, along with the most attractive, don't see themselves in the glamorous way others see them. For this reason famously successful people taking their own lives has become almost epidemic. It's also why many of the wealthiest and most influential are never satisfied with what they have amassed.

Self-doubt, driving either our need to prove ourselves or our acquiescence, is rooted in both nature and nurture. In his Pulitzer Prize Winner *The Denial of Death*, Ernest Becker shows just how profoundly the way we feel about ourselves is connected to our natural state. He writes that we are both out of nature and hopelessly in it—that we are dual, up in the stars and yet housed in a heart-pumping, breath-gasping body. He goes on to say, "Man is literally split in two: he has an awareness of his own splendid uniqueness in that he sticks out of nature with a towering majesty, and yet he goes back into the ground a few feet in order blindly and dumbly to rot and disappear forever."

It's on top of this foundation in nature—the contradiction between a mind that can fathom the stars and simultaneously knows it is going to become worm food—that nurture plays its part in the formation of our self-concept. We see ourselves through the eyes of others, esteeming ourselves in accordance with what they reflect back to us about ourselves. What they show us about ourselves during our years of growing up, whether accurate or grossly distorted by their own flawed self-perception, either drives us to prove ourselves or causes us to feel such a lack of self-worth that we allow ourselves to become downtrodden.

The habit of seeing ourselves through the eyes of others and evaluating ourselves based on how they respond to us originates with our mother and father, grandparents, siblings, and others who play a significant role in our upbringing. Not least among these are our teachers and religious guides.

The anxiety we have about ourselves as a result of our natural makeup, and the self-doubt transmitted by those who nurture us, explains why a woman puts up with males who abuse her, as well as why so many tolerate a boss who bullies us. For the same reason, a growing number of our young people knuckle under to a gang leader, whom they allow to practically own them. On a larger scale, it's why a nation permits a dictator to assume power and commit unspeakable atrocities.

If this were the whole picture, our situation would be bleak indeed. Happily, life has shown me that whether we struggle to establish our worth in the eyes of others or succumb to mediocrity and even abuse, the mindset that feeds both these polarities doesn't have the final say. We possess the capacity to transcend the limitations imposed on us by either nature or nurture. Each of us has the potential for expressing a higher consciousness that I often speak of as our "true" or "authentic" self.

I think of our true self in terms of our *essential* being. This is the individual we are beneath the insecure, self-doubting person produced by the impact of nurture on nature. It's the person we came into the world with the potential to be—the person we each are in essence, quite apart from the powerful influences that affect us.

I came into the world a dealmaker. Whether you think

of it as in my genes, or a feature of my spiritual self, it was an innate ability that was hijacked by a degree of self-doubt that all but drove me into my grave at the young age of 35. This drivenness was a manifestation of the unbalanced state I spoke of at the beginning of this chapter, an off-centered extreme that represented neither my essence nor my potential.

On the surface it appeared that I was driven to impress those who mattered to me—from a business point of view, particularly my father. As I explored more deeply, I came to see that in trying to impress others, it was actually *myself* I was trying to convince of my worth.

Beneath the way I strove to prove myself, I unconsciously believed that if I win the approval of others, I would at last feel good about myself. That this was largely unconscious didn't lessen the power it held over me.

I came to see that in even thinking along these lines—watching myself, evaluating my moves, critiquing my thoughts and emotions—I was *looking at myself,* which isn't at all the same as simply *being* oneself.

Looking at ourselves is a behavior we all engage in. It's reflected in the expressions we commonly use to speak of ourselves, such as when we refer to our "self-image," our "self-worth," or our "self-esteem." These each involve presenting a front to the world, which is quite different from simply being our genuine self…being *real* in everything.

What it takes to live in flow is authenticity, which is the state of being in which head and heart are united. It's impossible to be in flow if you aren't being genuine.

Our authentic self is often so different from the person we have learned to be in order to garner the approval of others that it can feel like there are two different people being expressed through us. There's the person we are in our essential being, our authentic self that we came into the world with the potential to be. Then there's the person we think we're supposed to be, the person we imagine ourselves as. To recognize this is potentially a life-changing insight.

When I speak of our "false self," I'm referring to the *picture* of ourselves we carry around in our head. This is the image we either seek to live up to or somehow can't seem to escape living down to.

It's this person we imagine ourselves to be, which is nothing more than a mirage of our own making, who's constantly trying to measure up. It's become common to refer to this image as our "ego," which we distinguish from who we are in our authentic self. The ego is a false *idea* of ourselves, an image we've adopted as camouflage for loss of awareness of our essence.

Ego is about seeing ourselves a certain way, then seeking to have others see us the way we wish them to see us, which we attempt to accomplish by coming across in a manner that aligns with our image of ourselves. It's about establishing validity in our *own* eyes, but doing so *as a spinoff* of feeling valid in the eyes of family, friends, society, and the world at large.

Ironically, were *we* convinced of our validity, we would have no need to convince anyone else of our validity. Without in any way suggesting we dismiss the praise of others or spurn their appreciation of us, the fact is that were we true to ourselves in every way, it wouldn't overly concern us what anyone thinks of us. There would be no self-doubt in need of reassurance from others.

When you have nothing to prove, you exude a trust and confidence that allows you to get clear in your own mind what you need to do, which you accomplish as an expression of *flow*. You don't worry about how you might come across. It doesn't concern you whether you are matching up to people's expectations. You don't even worry whether you are living up to your potential. You recognize that only ego concerns itself with such matters. The *real* you is content to just be the person you spontaneously find yourself to be in each moment.

Our drivenness to prove ourselves is the source of much of the insecurity, angst, and anger that afflicts us. We experience this drivenness only because we no longer know our true self. To not feel like we are "someone" eats away at us, since it's a basic need of *everyone* to know that their presence here is meaningful.

I grew up in the Islamic faith. The Arabic term "Islam" originates from the root *salem*, which essentially means "peace," implying a state that's the antithesis of being driven. *Salem* is related to the Hebrew word for peace, *shalom*. You hear this same root in the name of the city of Jeru*salem*. In Christianity, Jesus is said to be the Prince of Peace.

Despite religion's emphasis on being at peace with ourselves, and therefore with one another, the majority grow up learning to think of the divine not as a peaceful *presence,* but as *pressure.*

For thousands of years the city of Jerusalem was believed by many to stand at the center of the earth. Home to three of the world's major spiritual paths, it has known little peace during its long history, and yet it's very name embodies the concept of peace. The followers of Judaism, Christianity, and Islam, who number more than three and a half billion and make up practically half the world's population, all stress the importance of *finding inner peace, which is then mirrored in a peaceful external life.* Even though the Hindu and Buddhist spiritual paths are rooted elsewhere on the map than Jerusalem, they along with many other faiths emphasize *being at peace with ourselves and hence with one another.*

The reason we can't achieve our ideals either individually or collectively as a species lies in our doubts about whether we are good enough. As long as we don't feel good enough, we won't be at peace with either ourselves or one another. Personal inner peace and external communal and global peace are intrinsically linked to how we feel about ourselves.

Until our tendency to endlessly apologize for ourselves gets addressed, we're doomed to either struggle to prove ourselves in the eyes of others—and therefore hopefully but vainly in our own eyes—or to capitulate to whatever life happens to send our way.

The fact that my business decisions were being made based on the intuition that flowed from heart and mind functioning in unison didn't save me from the deleterious effects of the insecure state that my upbringing inadvertently layered over my authentic core.

The key to a meaningful life is to embrace changes and challenges in a calm, relaxed manner—something that's possible only to the degree that we are in tune with our essential being. From here, we move forward in trust, entering into a state of clarity, which in turn results in flow.

Before I was able to do this, I had to be brought face to face with what my driven ways were doing to me and how needless it was for me to operate in such a mode, when I could accomplish just as much and more from the state of flow. For this to happen my ego needed to cave in.

The path that brought me to the place I could embrace the way my life was unfolding led by way of hell, as I began describing in chapter one.

Dismantling my ego kicked off with going to ground zero financially during the aftermath of the Asian economic crisis of 1997. Next came the far greater crisis at the age of 35 when my health caved in as stage 3 cancer struck. This time it appeared it was "game over." The third crisis, which I experienced as the greatest blow of all, was my wife's decision to leave me.

I was to discover that crises come so that an authentic way of being can erupt into every facet of our everyday life, displacing the defensiveness of our ego. I say "erupt" because everything we typically count on to make us happy seems to get ruptured in this process.

I had to learn that when crises of a huge magnitude strike, *it's because our originally peaceful, joyous, loving self is seeking to break through our belief that we aren't good enough and need to somehow prove ourselves.*

If we embrace these crises instead of resisting them, the clarity that comes to us enables us not just to visit the state of flow now and then, but to live in flow. When this happens, any "happiness" we may have known can't hold a candle to the pure bliss, boundless joy, and unlimited love that become our ongoing state.

3

How to Be True to Yourself

Do we really need to go through repeated painful experiences to come to the place where we can trust in the goodness of life, embracing our own goodness without feeling we have something to prove?

Apparently some of us do. The reality is that few "get it" from a single pass. In some cases we have to endure experiences again and again, the purpose being to facilitate a rewiring of our neural circuits so that we begin to think and feel in a way that's true to who we are in our essence, whereby we are no longer aligned with the mask that's our ego.

The three distinct episodes that forced me to relinquish my ego each served a different purpose. Each in their turn took me to a deeper level of embracing the change that was occurring in my life. As piece by piece I felt my ego being dismantled, I discovered there could be no holding onto anything that had formerly seemed important to me. Through it all, a new clarity about my reason for being here was emerging.

Being a driven person actually helped me release my ego. After all, I had done my best. I had been doing my best all along. Apart from the fact it was in my nature to want to do my best, I was far too driven *not* to do my best.

To let go of the need to prove myself, which so evidently hadn't worked, was therefore a no-brainer. I was suffering so much as a result of my driven ways that there was nothing left *but* to let go. In each area of my life in which I was plunged into crisis, I bottomed out about as low as one can go and come out of it alive.

Generally patients with cancer go through an initial surgery, followed by chemo or radiation—and, if necessary, both. Had I taken this course, it would have been game over. I had germ cell tumors, as was the case with Lance Armstrong, which are 90% testicular in origin. Mine had metastasized so that I now had a tumor right in the center of my chest, in my sternum. Measuring 10x11x11 centimeters, it was roughly the size of a Rubric's cube. I also had a tumor the size of a tennis ball in my neck, together with no less than eight tumors in my lungs.

"Of course, you couldn't have a normal cancer like everybody else," an integrative doc who was counseling me remarked. "It wasn't enough for you to be part of the 90%." She was correlating the intensely driven component of my life with the seriousness of my cancer. To see the dots connected in this way became a vital component of my survival.

When she asked me how I was doing, I confessed, "I'm finished."

"So how were you before?"

"Going 100 miles an hour."

"And now?"

"Zero."

"And how do you feel physically?"

In truth, I felt like I was tumbling into a bottomless pit of emptiness. To come face to face with such a sensation within myself was terrifying. Still, it was clear that I was being asked to embrace this plunge into seeming oblivion, trusting that it would work for my ultimate good.

I told the integrative doc, "I feel like I'm on my knees."

"Perfect," she said.

"*What?*" I exclaimed.

"Perfect," she reiterated. "You're a Muslim, right? Bend down, prostrate yourself, and beg for your life."

"Excuse me?"

"Prostate yourself and beg for your life."

Hardly believing my ears, I objected, "This is what I'm paying you for?"

"Yes," she said unapologetically. "You're an arrogant human being. You think you can do it all yourself, so you never ask God for anything."

She was of course describing the mindset of the ego. I had to contemplate what she had said before responding, "You're right. I'm proud of what I've made of my life. I have an incredible wife, the most amazing two children, and until recently I was healthy with a seemingly infinite supply of energy. I had an exceptional upbringing and received an excellent education. I'm doing really well financially too. If I were to describe my life up until now, I guess I'd have to say, 'I'm flying.'"

"You're arrogant," she came back, hammering her point home, "and you don't ask anything from God because of your arrogance."

I was arrogant, and yet I hadn't actually considered myself arrogant. Perhaps at least in part that's why I weathered the first onslaught on my ego with only minimal difficulty. As I mentioned, the process of dismantling my ego got underway when my company was caught up in the aftermath of the Asian financial crisis. It was the late 1990s and I wasn't even 30. Although I was upset by the reversal my business went through, I had every confidence I would rebound.

As I shared with you in chapter one when I told you about my cancer, to trust we can rebound from a crisis is an important aspect of embracing what's occurring. But this trust in our ability to begin again needs to be rooted in our essence, not a repeat of ego. It isn't a matter of reassuring ourselves through positive thinking, which is what ego majors in. It's a much deeper sense that we are up for whatever life sends our way—joyously so. It involves an innate "knowing" that we have it within us to use any adverse situation to enhance the quality of our experience.

At the stage in my evolution when the financial crisis hit, I don't know that I would necessarily call the way I responded a *conscious* expression of trust. I believe that a basic trust in life is deeply rooted in each of us, even though our ability to exercise this trust may only be in an embryonic phase. In my case this trust took the form of "everything will be fine." I was young and had just married. When you're young, you tend to believe time is on your side and you can rebound.

The lesson that came out of this was a realization that a person can be wealthy, yet unexpectedly find their pile of cash wiped out by circumstances beyond their control. This of course is why one needs not only faith in one's ability to re-bound, but also the ability to trust in the overall benevolence of the universe—that life isn't out to "get us."

You will recall that the integrative doc told me I had never had to ask for any of the blessings life had showered on me. In the second crisis that befell me, all resistance to asking for help was shot to pieces and I was certainly asking now. It's as the 13th century Muslim poet Rumi remarked, "When the world pushes you to your knees, you're in the perfect position to pray."

Muslims pray five times a day. Because of my low energy, I needed a nap between each prayer. For nine months I lived from prayer to prayer, begging to be alive when the time for the next prayer rolled around.

Neither was this the only prayer I engaged in. Each and every day, I prayed extra to thank God that it was me going through what I was going through, not my wife, my chil-dren, my parents, or my brother. To watch a member of my family endure such cruel pain would have been unbearable. Although I hadn't allowed myself to connect deeply in a heart sense with those close to me, since this wasn't the way the family I grew up in did things, they were more important to me than my own life.

Albeit excruciatingly painful, the cancer did a most effective job of deepening my ability to express what I was feeling. Because of the number of tumors and their size, the doctors who were treating me had to shrink them first. To achieve this, I endured five days of chemo in a row, followed by two weeks at home. This was an extreme protocol of my own choosing.

My house was in order in terms of inheritance and succession planning, so I knew my family would be taken care of following my death. But with two little boys, I wasn't anywhere near ready to throw in the towel. Accepting that the cancer was probably going to claim my life was nowhere near as difficult as preparing to say goodbye to my boys.

One of the most painful aspects of my ordeal wasn't so much the prospect of facing death. With each of the many PET/CT scans I underwent, I spent time visualizing saying goodbye to all my loved ones. With deep sadness, I managed to say goodbye to my parents, my brother, my cousin, and even my wife. But when I attempted to visualize saying goodbye to my boys, who were only one and three, my body wouldn't allow me to go there. It was way too painful to even contemplate.

It was for this reason that I asked my doctors to give me the absolute maximum dose of chemotherapy permissible, despite the excruciating suffering each dose caused. "If I'm to die in peace, I have to be able to look my two boys in their eyes, assuring them, 'Baba did his best, but the Big Boss decided otherwise.'"

During the five consecutive days of chemo, I lost five kilos. For the entire next week at home, I could taste nothing because of the metals in the chemo. Since I was forced to eat so as not to lose even more weight, I had to imagine how the food tasted. Thankfully my ability to taste always returned during the second week at home, enabling me to regain the lost weight from the week of treatment. This routine of five days of chemo followed by two weeks of regaining lost weight was repeated four times, for a total of twenty rounds of chemo. These were followed by three surgeries.

Every time I returned home after my five days of chemo, as well as being in immense physical distress, I was so mentally and emotionally depleted that I had a huge resistance to ever returning to the hospital. I would get on my knees, with my head on my wife's lap, wailing as I begged her to promise not to take me back for further treatment. Each time, she remained silent, as she knew that going back was the only realistic option. I would then spend two weeks at home, with my two little boys giving me the courage to be blasted with a further five rounds of chemo.

I had begun to think that God must derive pleasure from torturing me, which is why I used to say, "God, have you had enough entertainment? Do you still need me to suffer so you can entertain yourself further? Or can you go find someone else to entertain you?" With blow after blow raining down on me, I felt like Job in the Jewish Scriptures.

My integrative doc's coup de grâce stunned me. "And let's be quite clear," she said, "you created all of this."

I was like, "Do I really look that warped?" It was initially hard to swallow that it wasn't God who was inflicting such pain on me, but that I had brought this suffering on myself.

My agony caused me to engage in serious reflection, a practice I've continued ever since. The intuitive doc's insights got me thinking in a new vein. Could I really be so masochistic that I had actually gone out of my way to screw up my happiness?

I had to own that it *was* largely my own fault that I was in this life-threatening state. I had been so driven to prove myself, working in my businesses to the exclusion of almost everything else, that I *gave* myself cancer. My unbalanced way of being had depleted my reserves to the point of practically signing my death warrant.

I traveled six months of the year and worked every day until around 8 p.m. When I wasn't traveling, I didn't socialize, didn't go in for parties, didn't go to dinner with friends or business acquaintances. My time was spent at home. My life was focused on either work or home, travel or home. Except that if you're on the phone and you're aggressive and angry, even shouting into the phone, just how "at home" are you?

I did things with the intention of them being a "we" activity, but it came off as "I." This is because even when I was present, I wasn't actually present, tuned into my family and their needs. If you were to look at photos from this time in my life, you'd see one of my sons in my arms and me on a call.

We'd be on a boat in Thailand, with Kazim enjoying a guava while I was on my Blackberry.

It wasn't that my authentic self was completely absent, for it was the source of my business genius. It's just that, unless I was working, I had picked up the habit of overriding other aspects of my real self. True self is present in some measure in all of us—we don't consist entirely of ego. Even those of us whose ego is extremely dense catch who we really are peeking from behind our mask in certain aspects of life.

As the months went by and I was in and out of hospital, I came to the realization that to have any real chance of coming back from the cancer that wracked my body, it would take more than the extreme medical treatment I was receiving. Vital as this intervention was, it alone couldn't save me.

As the integrative doc I had hired was showing me, I needed to go through a huge shift in how I functioned in my everyday life. There could be no more arrogance that stemmed from my endless need to prove myself—in other words, no more of the ego that had driven me into this predicament. I also realized that if I survived, I would have the cancer to thank for saving my life, since it had spared me from dropping dead of a heart attack as a result of my driven ways.

It seemed that life was giving me a second chance. Was I going to continue living other people's definition of success? Or would I seize the opportunity to live in a manner that was more in line with my own essence, with my head and heart united to guide me in living a balanced life for a change?

So serious was my predicament that I knew that from this

point onwards, I would need to be guided by *what it means to be real in everything*.

4

Trust Replaces Ego

To realize that the ego is nothing but a mirage is a pre-requisite for freeing ourselves from the false sense of self it imparts. Plunging all the way down to our core, we are surprised to discover that the seeming emptiness within us is *neither bottomless nor empty.*

It was when I hit rock bottom that I ran slap bang into my *forgotten authentic self.*

There are two phases to shifting out of ego into authentic-ity. When I really "got" just how catastrophically my health had failed and that my need to prove I was good enough was the principal reason, I realized I was utterly helpless. This realization allowed me to move through the first phase of per-mitting my ego to dissolve without putting up a whole lot of resistance.

To get a picture of what happens when you make the shift from ego to authentic self, think of punching a hole in the Michelin blimp. You watch with alarm as the advertising em-blazoned on the side of the blimp crumples in full view of everyone. That's what it initially feels like when one's ego deflates.

I don't want you to confuse what was happening to me with the idea advocated by various faiths and gurus—and today increasingly popular in self-help circles—that this is about what people refer to as "surrender." As I touched on earlier, various faith paths—especially the three Abrahamic faiths—have long advocated surrender to what they imagine to be the "will of God."

I want to be perfectly clear that *to embrace a situation is fundamentally different from what most of us mean by surrender.*

When I hear people speak of surrender, they almost always think we are supposed to surrender to our *situation,* as if some superior being had decreed such a situation should befall us. It doesn't seem to occur to us that what life might really be asking of us is to open up to *something within ourselves that's asking to be recognized and embraced.*

As the ego deflates, phase two of moving beyond this mode of functioning requires us to *embrace the powerful person we truly are.* We awaken to the incredible individual who has been in hiding beneath our carefully groomed self-image. As we quit "advertising" ourselves, which is the ego's blimpish way of going about things, we instead embark on simply *being* ourselves.

The dissolving of our ego is fundamentally different from capitulating to our circumstances. If you read the stories of people who attribute their success to having surrendered to life, you'll find that in reality this success resulted from becoming highly proactive. They learned the art of becoming quiet, which isn't at all the same as capitulation. This enabled them to sense opportunities, then seize those opportunities, often working hard for them. They didn't float idly downstream assuming a superior being or "higher reality" would take care of everything. They took responsibility for their success.

Why would you capitulate to adverse circumstances? The only reasons might be that you've either run out of gas emotionally or you've bought into the idea that an intelligence bigger than you is running the show, and see yourself as simply along for the ride.

If you happen to have bought into the belief that things are either "meant" or "not meant" to be, I refer you to a quip by Stephen Hawking: "I have noticed that even people who claim everything is predetermined and that we can do nothing to change it, look before they cross the road."

When we allow things to just "happen," which surrender implies, we all know what tends to happen...

On the other hand, dethroning our ego isn't something we have to work at. To embrace life with authenticity automatically dethrones ego. It's this powerful authentic self that the changes and challenges we experience have the potential to bring out. It happens as we choose to respond to the hints we receive of the truly powerful person we are in our essence. Unlike surrender, there's nothing laissez faire about embracing life.

As we respond to the hints we receive—the inklings we get of what we are here to do during our lifetime—we experience confirmation that we're on the right track. There emerges from deep within an inexplicable lightness. In fact, I suggest that whenever we are being authentic, life always has this light touch to it. As this lightness arises in us, we find ourselves becoming free of everything around us to which we formerly clung for an identity.

The heaviness of ego is dispersed in the same way darkness is banished from a room. No effort is required to "surrender" the darkness. Instead we need only flip the light switch. Our attempts to surrender to situations are effort on the part of the ego to preserve itself. "See," it crows, "look what I did."

This may sound surprising, but my experience is that when you embrace even an illness instead of fighting it, you feel elated. This is because by embracing instead of resisting, you spontaneously find yourself moving out of a fearful state into trust. Insecurity, anxiety, doubt, and other negative emotions are replaced with feelings of peacefulness, hope, joyfulness, and love. Were you to tell others about how you feel, they would think you're nuts because, well, aren't you dying? You have this disease that's eating you up. How can you possibly feel incredible?

Through my company Qineticare, I work with many cancer patients all over the world. Once a person is in remission, if I sense they are ready to truly open up so that we can explore any emotional and other factors that may have contributed to their cancer, I say to them, "When you're in a place of absolute trust, you feel so light, so nothing, that you resemble a butterfly."

Unless they had been there themselves, it's doubtful anyone could have understood my trust in the universe while I was dealing with cancer. That I came to regard what was happening to me as the best thing that could have befallen me at this stage in my life would mystify most. Knowing that they were unlikely to understand where I was coming from, I preferred that few visit me while I was ill.

There was an additional reason I kept visitors to a minimum. I realized that if I was to give myself a chance of recovering, every step I took had to spring from deep awareness and crystal clear intentionality. For such awareness and clarity to develop, I required silence.

To tap into my personal GPS at this critical juncture, I needed to access the stillness that resided in my essence. Only then could I gain the clarity and intentionality that were essential for my recovery. To this end, I found I required a great deal of silence. If we are to gain clarity, most of the different spiritual paths advocate we enter into stillness through one means or another. My chosen path at this time was to be alone much of the time.

Humans have long tended to associate the divine with dramatic events in nature. But the story of Elijah in the Hebrew scriptures offers us a different insight into how God is revealed to us. Elijah is discouraged and wants God to show himself as a means of reassurance that he's on the right track. He's told to stand on the mountain to which he has journeyed. Then the drama begins.

First there is a wind, perhaps a tornado or hurricane, so powerful that it sends rocks crashing down to be broken apart. Following the windstorm there is an earthquake. After the earthquake comes a firestorm, likely a huge fireworks display of lightning. In none of these does God appear to Elijah.

Only when the drama is over does Elijah perceive the divine presence, which comes in the form of what the traditional translation describes as "a still small voice." The New Revised Standard Version gives the sense more accurately when it says that there came *"a sound of sheer silence."*

The expression "a sound of sheer silence" points to the absolute stillness in which the infinite mystery we call God, Allah, Buddha consciousness, Brahman, and so forth abides. It equates to what a later writer in the Christian tradition speaks of as "the peace of God, which surpasses all understanding."

Although my background is Muslim, not Christian, I have learned that the core truths are available through pretty much all spiritual paths, each of which we can learn from. It isn't so much that these truths become our guide, but that they awaken us to our *own internal guidance system*, which becomes the source of our clarity.

This sheer stillness that comes with clarity is palpable. You can feel it. It's what we experience at moments when we are completely transported out of our mundane state by the rapture of the moment, such as when we become one with a sunset. It's the stillness we feel afloat on the vastness of the ocean. It's the silence of a night sky ablaze with galaxies when we are in the wilderness away from all artificial light and sound. It's the sense of sheer wonder that can arise when two people become so enraptured in sexual love that their boundaries melt away for a time and they know an exquisite oneness.

At such a moment, there are simply no words, no thoughts that can express what we are experiencing. We enjoy a wordless clarity, a knowing that doesn't require thought—features of a transcendent aliveness in which the depth of feeling we experience is indescribable.

What does it take for a person to become quiet, truly quiet to the point they don't know what to say and can at last access the clarity that resides within?

The stillness I had opted for during my hospital stays was about to be intensified, this time not by choice. Following my twenty rounds of chemotherapy, I went in for a scheduled follow up during which my doctor drew blood to run various tests. When the results came through he said to me, "Did you walk in here? You shouldn't be able to walk. Your blood work is so awful, I need to put you in isolation immediately."

"I'm not going anywhere," I retorted.

"You don't have a choice," he informed me. "If somebody sneezes on you or you come into contact with any kind of infection, the consequences may well be catastrophic."

I had endured so much hospital time that I couldn't imagine going back, and yet within minutes I was in a week-long isolation. No family or friends were allowed to visit, although

I did talk my doctor into allowing my wife to accompany me at my own risk.

Whenever hospital staff entered the room, they had to don special protective clothing. Despite this, the worst happened. One night I began running a fever, which is the last thing you want when you're in isolation. The nursing staff who were monitoring me told me, "We'll wait two hours. If the fever doesn't come down, the doctor will blast you with all kinds of drugs, to the point we can't guarantee you will be conscious." I realized that I was in a situation from which there might be no return. If there was ever a need to say my goodbyes, this would surely be it.

During those two hours, my wife and I didn't speak a word to each other. I knew the situation could go sideways really quickly, so my mind was completely quiet with no thoughts coming to me. Thankfully the fever began to recede, but I had never been this quiet in my life. I didn't even know how to begin saying my goodbyes had such been necessary, even though I had rehearsed many times during the PET/CT scans. Nothing was coming to me.

We are told that Elijah "heard" the sheer silence I was now experiencing. Not in an audible way, but with a silent clarity that was unmistakable. You might say that the message came through loud and clear. That's because this simple and uncomplicated knowing is unlike any other state we experience.

The sound of sheer silence speaks the language of realness, which is quite distinct from our jumbled and often confusing thoughts and emotions. It's utterly different in character from all the voices in our head that clamor for our attention, let alone the passions that seize us and cause us to make irrational moves.

When we are attuned to this inner stillness, we just sense whatever it is we need to know. There is absolute intuitive clarity, which results in the kind of unwavering intentionality that facilitates action that flows.

Unlike my first experience of releasing the drivenness of ego and taking fledgling steps into a state of trust during the Asian financial crisis, I would describe my stage three cancer as something that was carried off in a relatively graceful manner. This was because my ability to embrace my situation was an expression of head and heart united.

This was me as a whole person taking action, the authentic me I found hidden beneath the layers of ego that had driven me to try to prove I was good enough. I may have been incapacitated, but at least it was the *real* me that was incapacitated, since I was incapable of being my big ego any longer.

Instead of continuing to be driven by the need to prove myself, I had been handed an opportunity to have my whole life unfold from the flow that accompanies being truly present in our life. I didn't just experience the zone momentarily but was learning to allow each and every decision to emerge from that place deep within us where intelligence and feeling no longer clash but function synergistically to bring us the maximum fulfillment life is capable of providing us with.

Little did I know that before I could enter fully into a life in which all that we engage in is experienced as meaningful, instead of in the mediocre manner that's the norm for the majority, a further episode of head and heart replacing ego lay ahead. It was to last three years and be the most painful experience of all—yes, even beyond the agonizing eleven months of cancer treatment.

People close to me assured me, "You've gone through so much, there must be incredible things around the corner." Given the pain I was in, such words weren't of much comfort to me at the time—although deep down I prayed that what they were saying might turn out to be true.

"Enough is enough," one person remarked, laughing in sympathy with me. "It's time the diamond polishing was over and you were simply allowed to sparkle like you were meant to." Her words were encouraging, though I think both of us knew that the polishing never really ends. It just shifts gears, from the experience of shedding deficits from our past to embracing assets that represent our authentic self.

5

"Till Death Do Us Part?"

The third crisis I experienced forced me to face up to my failure to be present with people, really present. To learn how to be with others, I first needed to learn how to truly be with *myself*, free of any sense of needing to prove myself. I needed to experience total self-acceptance, embracing myself in every way. The route to this would be the painful path of separation and eventual divorce.

It's crazy how emotions can create the most incredible experiences, then suddenly disrupt our ecstasy by plunging us into pain beyond imagination. But crazy or not, it's a fact of life to which all too many of us can attest. We can't control emotions and we certainly can't predict them. They arise when and as they arise, unbidden.

Our fifteenth wedding anniversary fell during white truffle season, so my wife and I went to lunch at Otto e Mezzo. Whereas most people invest in the stock market, bonds, or real estate, we had been investing in precious stones. I had purchased a special stone without my wife knowing, so I gave it to her to mark this occasion. It was a dazzling fusion of blue and green hues, reminiscent of the changing colors of the ocean.

Despite this huge gesture on my part, we departed the restaurant having decided that in a month we would separate. Following lunch, I chose to go for a walk instead of immediately entering the apartment, crying and begging as I walked.

At the apartment, my wife stepped into a home adorned with the most gorgeous array of flowers you could imagine. One of Hong Kong's foremost florists had decorated the entrance, dining room, my wife's study, and the bedroom with a huge assortment of the finest flowers on the market. I had spent thousands of dollars to try to show her what she meant to me. When I eventually returned to the apartment, if she thanked me, I don't remember it. We had clearly reached the end of the line.

Things had begun to come apart late one evening when, as I turned in for the night, I gestured to my wife that I would like to hold her. To my complete surprise she responded, "I can't do this anymore. I'm sorry, but I don't love you and can't give myself to you."

The shock was immense. The only thing I knew to do was roll over to hide the overwhelming pain I was in.

In the days following this announcement, I was beyond all my coping skills, in a realm of distress I don't begin to have words to describe. I initially blamed myself, telling myself I had failed not only my wife but also my children. What kind of human being was I if I couldn't hold a marriage together for their wellbeing?

How does one face up to such a catastrophic failure? My self-doubt, insecurity, and failure to really believe in myself were on the front burner.

Interrogating myself was particularly painful because my oldest son had an especially hard time with my divorce. He blamed me, believing I caused it because of the way I was as a person—in other words, because of me being *me,* meaning the ego version of myself. Even though his mother made the decision to leave, in my son's mind I was the catalyst. "She *had* to leave," he reasoned, "because she was with *you.*"

It took time for me to really comprehend what my son was saying. At the end of a workshop one time, the teacher conducting the workshop gave out rocks he had collected on one of his walks. Whereas everybody else's were smooth, my rock was spiky. "Are you surprised?" the teacher asked, "because I'm not." This was someone who had begun helping me a month after I was diagnosed with cancer and knew everything about me all the way back to childhood.

Even when we recognize that a relationship has come to an end at least in part as a result of our own doing, it's nevertheless a disappointment to have planned your future around someone only to find they're not going to be there to share it with you after all. I cried way more and begged way more than I did even when I was within an inch of dying from cancer, which is really bizarre when you think about it. But my upbringing had drilled into me that the woman I married was to be my partner "till death do us part."

We can never know whether two people will stay together through thick and thin. Marriage is always somewhat of a gamble, no matter how well we do our homework. Suppose we give it everything we've got, really studying and working to create a relationship that will accompany us throughout our lives. There's just one problem—and it's a potential Achilles' Heel. Unless feelings are arising from the deep currents of our authentic being, they don't have longevity. They occur in the moment, moment by moment, and they can shift, ultimately changing our course in life. This is what occurred on my wife's part.

No matter how much we try to ensure a match is a good one, there's simply no way to know it will work over the long term. It's because of this that the way I grew up, I was conditioned culturally to play it "safe" when it came to getting married. Supposedly to make life smoother, I was guided to marry within my culture. When my former father-in-law asked his daughter to consider me as a possible husband, her reaction was that I was too old because we had an eight-year age gap. But as he ticked the boxes, the fact that I was a Muslim, prayed, didn't drink, was educated, made a good living, and was from a good family made me a good match in his eyes.

I joked with my mother, who was ticking the boxes and pressuring me to marry, "Just Fed Ex her and I'll accept the package." The way my mother looked at life, you were of a certain age so you got married. It's just another thing you did along the way.

On neither my intended's side nor mine was there any thought of looking beyond what society considers a success. And how is that success defined? By ticking the boxes:

- What family is he from? Tick.
- Is he educated? Tick.
- Is he making a good living? Tick.
- Does he pray? Tick.
- Does he have a good reputation? Tick.

After you've ticked all the boxes, you have someone who fits the family's profile of an ideal spouse. These may be important factors, but they are no guarantee that a marriage will have lifelong longevity.

Did my wife and I make a wrong choice? I believe it was right for both of us *at that time* in our lives. An extremely conservative individual recommended her to me, then someone with a truly modern Western perspective made the same recommendation independently. If this woman was getting a green light from trusted individuals with the most conservative perspective on the one hand and the most progressive on the other, she had to be special, which of course is why I agreed to meet and eventually marry her.

I took my best shot, had many great years that included the birth of two wonderful sons, and finally had to embrace a divorce I had no control over. When my wife was ready to execute the divorce, my back went out. It was a reflection of my emotional state, mirroring the fact I was losing the woman who had been my support system. When I couldn't get out of bed, I asked my assistant to help me, but it was to no avail.

I tried dozens of times, but the excruciating nature of the pain defeated me. My helper finally decided she had to call my wife and ask her to come.

When my wife arrived, being a reiki master and having engaged in a great deal of energy work, she quickly realized that since she and I were energetically connected, the problem with my back lay in how my support system was about to collapse. As we talked, it turned out that the moment she had entered the attorney's office to execute the divorce was the exact moment my back had given way, so powerful are our emotions and so deep is our connection with one another. The consequence was that we agreed to delay the whole process of divorce by a year to help me recover. A year later, she didn't bring the matter up. We ended up taking three years to move from separation to divorce.

When the divorce finally happened, for some time I circled around time and again to the sense of not being good enough. But as I allowed these thoughts and emotions to percolate, ultimately I came to see that it wasn't about me but about her.

Growing apart is something that happens to a lot of people. We go years in a relationship imagining we will be together forever, only to awaken to the fact that at our core we sense we don't belong together—and, in some cases, never really did love each other in the deep, heart kind of way. Emotional attachment, which is quite different from the deep currents of the heart, can bind us together for a long time, even a lifetime. It can also mask the fact that how we truly feel is very different. To face up to this is a positive step, not a misstep. It's to address a deficit that holds the potential of becoming an asset.

Even as my wife was getting in touch with what she really knew and felt, so also the process was underway within me. I was well versed in imposing on others, directing them, taking charge, and caring for their material needs and physical wellbeing, but not in simply being "with" them on an equal footing. I needed to embrace my capacity for real presence and the even deeper caring that it facilitates. The way life would bring this about came as a complete surprise.

Once we made the decision to separate, I moved into a service apartment, crying as I went back and forth between the apartment and my home each day. It was a horrid experience, an ongoing reminder of how my heart had been ripped open. I felt so unbelievably lonely, for I was no longer welcome in my own home. What had been my place of succor now felt alien to me.

Aloneness and loneliness aren't the same. To be alone at times is a reality of life, but in and of itself it isn't at all painful. Loneliness can be painful, agonizingly so, because it's a churning sea of emotion produced by our thoughts—an illusion that has nothing to do with reality.

There is no ultimate loneliness in the world. How could there be when we are all part of an intricately interwoven reality, connected up in more ways than we can imagine? Life is a vast tapestry, with each of us its threads. Only as this reality becomes buried beneath thoughts and emotions that don't represent the true state of things can we ever feel lonely.

In *Walden*, Henry David Thoreau writes of a day when, in the midst of a gentle rain, he became aware of "such sweet and beneficent society in nature, in the very pattering of the drops, and in every sound and sight...an infinite and unaccountable friendliness all at once like an atmosphere sustaining me. Every little pine needle expanded and swelled with sympathy and befriended me."

To sense our oneness with being, to feel ourselves not only a part of an infinite whole but the very expression of that which gives rise to the whole–is to know loneliness no longer. But until we are aware of this connection between ourselves and the oneness that unites all of reality, we are strangers to ourselves. And when we are strangers to our own reality, we are strangers to one another. We may be alongside each other, but we are truly quite unknown to and by each other and experience a constant need to prove ourselves to the other.

If we all get together in our alienation from our true selves, we are just Sergeant Pepper's Lonely Hearts Club Band. We are a pool of emotionally isolated souls. Some twosomes or groups squabble, which is a technique for taking our minds off our inner sense of isolation. Keep arguing, and you don't have to feel alone. Others agree on everything, never arguing or falling out because each party is careful not to be real, which would instantly end the illusion of unbroken togetherness. Whether in combat or in compromise, we are hiding from our inner alienation from our authentic self—what we really know in our head and feel in our heart.

How to assuage the inner loneliness that stems from alienation from our true self? We must touch something within ourselves that doesn't know loneliness and that therefore can satisfy our yearning. We must become aware that, beneath the isolation of ego, our authentic self is intrinsically connected to the whole of reality through head and heart united.

I saw that the alienation I had experienced had nothing to do with the fact this was once the home my wife and I shared with our boys. It was an alienation within my own being, a further aspect of my alienation from my authentic self.

My wife and I had a deep connection, but evidently on her part it wasn't the sort of connection she wanted in a marriage, a reality she was finally facing up to. She had grown up in the years we were together raising a family. During the process, she had discovered what was more true to her deepest desires, and I applaud her courage in making a change that reflected where she was.

Each of us grows into who we truly are in our deeper being at our own pace. There's no formula, no timetable. As clarity dawns in us, we must each go with our *own* flow. It took time for me to realize that my wife's decision to leave was doing me a favor.

You've no doubt heard the aphorism, "Feel it to heal it." Living in the service apartment, there was no way to avoid the full impact of my wife's decision and the intense loneliness it triggered. The only way forward was to embrace it. And as I did so, a metamorphosis happened within me.

Five months after moving out, while my wife and the boys were on vacation in Canada, I received a surprise. Entering what had been my home and finding no one there, I was surprised to discover that it didn't feel alien to me at all. Neither did it feel empty, nor I lonely. In fact it felt really good.

When I spoke to my spiritual masters about this surprising reversal of what I had been anticipating, they commented, "We told you from day one that your wife should move out, not you. It was her decision to take a different path that would ultimately lead her away from the home. But you couldn't hear this back then."

I had told myself I moved into the service apartment because I didn't want the boys to be separated from their mother. Little did I know that the real reason was self-rejection. The guilt associated with having failed at my marriage had led to whether I was "good enough" yet again raising its ugly head. Now at last I was learning to embrace myself, replete with my shortcomings, instead of judging and rejecting myself.

When my wife and the boys returned it was during Ramadan. "Why are you still here?" she asked as we had a bite to eat one morning before fasting.

"This is my home and I'm here to be with my family," I replied.

"Are you saying you want me to move out?" she inquired.

"That has to be your choice," I said, finding my courage after all these months. Feeling good enough about myself to declare my true feelings, I finally experienced the lightness mentioned in an earlier chapter, a lightness that confirms when we are being authentic.

For the next two years my ex slept in the service apartment. Other than this, we made every day as normal as possible for the boys. She was there when they came home from school, we ate meals together, we put the boys to sleep together, and we spent our weekends together. At night she went back to the service apartment, returning most mornings in time for the boys to see her before I dropped them off to school. Given that I was still dependent on her for my happiness, I too was glad to see her each day.

Life urges us to move through situations in order to move on. When we embrace a situation, trusting that our path will emerge and waiting for clarity to arise within us, in due course we quite naturally flow into the next phase of our life. That said, some of us love the person we share so many precious memories with for the rest of our days. It's just that our alienation from ourselves often leads us to caricature the person. We don't know how else to deal with their former role in our life, so we turn them into an enemy.

Although my former wife and I weren't destined to spend the rest of our lives together, it didn't negate the bond between us—and nor should it. On one occasion I presented her with a hypothetical situation: "Suppose you were in the middle of nowhere and you could only make one quick call, who would you call?"

"I would call you," she said without hesitation.

I countered, "Why wouldn't you call your sister, your father, or your dear friend? Why would you call me when you don't want to be with me?"

There was no logic to her answer, but every time it was the same: "I'm sorry, but I can't help how I feel."

How can you argue with what someone genuinely feels? All you can do is allow, so that you deal with the pain yourself and don't take it out on the one who is just being honest about their feelings.

When you rely on your thoughts, they can really run you in circles. When you rely on what many label as their heart, which is generally their emotions, these too make no sense, turbulent as they can be. We need to allow our authentic self to lead us. It's about being real, with our brain in gear and our feelings attuned.

For this to happen requires full input on all fronts. Our deeper being doesn't function in isolation from the rest of reality. We consider everything, calmly allowing ourselves to come to the wisest decision possible at a given moment. Whether we would make that same decision at a later time isn't even in the picture, because that would be to formulate a concept instead of simply being present in *this* moment.

6

What Do We Actually Mean by

"Head and Heart?"

It's become popular in self-help circles and counseling situations to separate head from heart, usually pitting one against the other. You've perhaps heard people accuse someone of always relying on their head, with advice given to "follow your heart for a change."

It's true that many indulge in a lot of thought and are largely out of touch with their feelings. In recent decades, to bring heart into the equation has become a popular theme of novels and movies, along with the therapist's couch.

The question of whether head and heart are really two separate entities moved to center stage for me when I was introduced to a woman who at first sight I knew was exceptional.

Since my eighteen-year marriage had ended, I hadn't dated. For a long time I didn't even consider my friends' urging me to "get out there." I was well aware that for a relationship to be successful, there has to be a lot more than physical attraction, intelligence, and certain interests in common. There has to be something *magical.*

When this woman came into my life, the magic was all there. In so many ways she was everything I could wish for in a partner. Was I going to spend the rest of my life single, or was I going to allow myself the pleasure of this very special woman's company through the years?

Although I was entranced by the sheer magic of the relationship, I couldn't avoid a measure of skepticism that such could work at this point in my life. The timing felt all wrong. Not only did this woman live on another continent, but she was in her mid thirties and had never been married. I on the other hand was in my late forties with two sons who were entering their teens. What I considered to be common sense told me, "Don't do this. She's too young and the whole thing is too complicated."

My thoughts argued back and forth, presenting me with pros and cons, which I analyzed from every angle, at times with the help of those I was close to. My emotions pulled me one way, then my thoughts the other. How to resolve this conundrum? How could I know the right course?

This relationship was destined to play an important role in clarifying the issue of head and heart. What exactly do we mean when we speak of our head or our heart?

When it came to business decisions, I pretty much always *knew* what to do when an opportunity presented itself. I had a sense for which markets to go into, which products to buy and ship, and who to add to my team. I investigated the ins and outs of a situation, recognized the potential downsides as well as the possible gains, and quickly came to a clear decision.

My ability to rapidly come to intuitive conclusions where business dealings were concerned had always been second nature to me. I thrived on such clarity because this aspect of my makeup was encouraged, supported, and reinforced by my family while I was growing up. Whatever downsides I may have picked up from my upbringing, as we all do to some extent, my ability to make intuitive business decisions shone like a beacon. I was a natural at it, using both head and heart, which enabled me to trust myself and move forward based on the kind of clarity that supports flow.

It's not often recognized that it's natural for us to use head and heart together. Only as a result of the influence of family and society during our formative years do we in varying degrees abandon this innate aspect of our makeup.

It's clear that much of my success was due to the fact that not only did I have a keen mind, but my heart had always been in my businesses. Not too many on the planet have envisioned, created, and run business enterprises involving hundreds of millions of dollars. I have been blessed to be one of the few to whom such success has been entrusted. By my thirties I was responsible for over 10,000 employees, operating in seven countries in war-torn Africa and five in Eastern Europe, along with maintaining buying offices in Dubai, Paris, and Hong Kong.

My success was the result of head and heart functioning in unison. The only drawback was that my need to prove I was good enough as a result of the self-doubt I had picked up along the way caused me to be driven. This was where ego barged in.

But when it came to this incredible woman, such trust in my ability to see the way forward as I did in my businesses was absent. Why was the clarity I enjoyed in business absent in the matter of this relationship? This dilemma brought the issue of head and heart onto front burner.

When I tried to suppress my skeptical thoughts and just "follow my heart," which is what everyone said you should do where love is concerned, I found I couldn't confidently make a decision either to go with or turn away from this relationship.

After some time and our plans for the future not shaping up all that well, I came to understand that suppressing my logic wasn't at all what I needed to do, and neither could I rely on what I imagined to be my heart as a safe guide. It was increasingly apparent that the assumed rivalry between head and heart was a straw man. Abandoning my common sense and letting my emotions run the show was doing me in.

I needed to recalibrate. The whole idea of head *versus* heart was clearly mistaken—the result of a failure to understand the difference between the mind and our countless nonsensical thoughts on the one hand, and our real feelings and our often turbulent and frequently contradictory emotions on the other.

Instead of intuiting my way forward as I did in my business life, I was stewing emotionally to the point of making myself miserable. And therein lay the key to making sense of this whole conundrum. I was stewing *emotionally,* while simultaneously tangled up in *my thoughts about* the situation.

It dawned on me that when people talk about using their head, they tend to mean listening to their *thoughts,* which may not be at all the same as tuning into the insight and wisdom provided by their mind. When they talk about using their heart, they generally mean their *emotions*, which may even contradict their true *feelings.*

I was learning that society in general seems to have this whole issue of head versus heart muddled up. We say something is our "head," when it isn't the logical aspect of our mind we're referring to at all. At the same time, we call our emotions "feelings," when in reality there may be a huge difference between an emotion we are experiencing and what we are feeling deep down.

Perhaps you imagine yourself to be a thinking person. However, really using your mind is totally different from having thoughts. I'm quite sure you have lots of thoughts, as do we all. But if you look more closely at the endless parade of thoughts that pass through your head, you'll discover that instead of actively "thinking" these thoughts, the vast majority of your thoughts simply pop up from seemingly nowhere. So rather than "having thoughts," it might be more accurate to say that most of the time *our thoughts have us.*

Thoughts are just thoughts and don't necessarily represent

our analytical powers, intelligence, logic, insights, intuition, or wisdom—the qualities I'm referring to when I speak of the need to use our "head."

Some of the thoughts we have are just plain ridiculous. The wise person allows them to come and go without either dwelling on them or fighting them. We accept that they just *are*, a feature of existence that's common to all humans—"idiots in our house," as a mystic once called them. Don't worry—if you think really crazy thoughts, so too do the rest of us. If we paid attention to all the thoughts that enter our head, we'd soon find ourselves unable to function.

Just as our thoughts can lead us down the garden path, so too can our emotions, which aren't at all what real "heart" is. In fact emotions tend to block the true desires and deeper feelings of the heart. Consequently if you follow only your emotions, you're likely to complicate your life. One minute you'll be set on going in a particular direction, whereas the next it's "all change." You can be so "in love" with someone, but moments later when they do something you don't like, you can find yourself yelling, "I hate you! I never want to see you again."

To get a really clear picture of the difference between emotions and feelings, consider a couple who hire a babysitter for Valentine's Day and go out for a romantic dinner. Their plan is to return home for a passionate encounter. But on the drive back from the restaurant, they get into a disagreement over whether their daughter is to go to a private school or public school when she graduates from elementary to junior high.

The argument escalates to where the two end up on opposite sides of the bed with a wide no-man's land between them. What are they *feeling?*

Both are having a lot of thoughts about just how upset they are with their partner. Both are intensely emotionally reactive. "He hurt my feelings. How could he say that?" the wife tells herself, while the husband is stewing over why his wife can't understand that he has other financial obligations. There'll be no lovemaking that night, nor for the next several nights.

Where emotion is high, thoughts simultaneously run wild. But neither thoughts nor emotions represent either heart or head. Emotion and thoughts at a time like this are in fact the opposite of what the heart "feels" and the mind "knows."

The emotion unleashed in such an argument screams, "Get away from me. Stay on your own side of the bed—in fact, go sleep on the couch! Don't dare touch me. Don't even say a word!"

But what's the *feeling* beneath the emotion? The feeling, which is being eclipsed by the force of the reaction, is that both wish this argument had never happened and that they could resolve it and reconnect.

"Stay away from me" the thoughts of both shriek. "Why did you have to spoil a lovely evening? See if I ever go to dinner with *you* again!" In contrast the mind knows they aren't about to split up over this. It knows they'll heal the rift—even as the emotion growls "just not yet!"

Says the heart, "I wish you'd reach out. I wish I could

reach out. I hate feeling upset with you like this."

But the emotion counters angrily, "You better not reach out—or I'll slap your hand away. And *I'm* not going to reach out because you might slap my hand away."

I also want to be clear that heart isn't simply an awareness that something *feels* good. Lots of emotionally driven actions can feel good in the short term. It might feel good to be in free fall from a plane—but if you fail to pull the ripcord, you are going to end all feeling and all thought permanently.

When people imagine their heart is leading them to do something potentially destructive of their happiness, such as getting involved in an affair, it isn't their heart that's leading at all—it's emotional neediness. Neither is it their mind that's agreeing to the affair, but a train of illogical thought that seeks to justify the emotion's choice by arguing, "Why not? No one need ever know."

Thoughts and emotions can come together with such force that they totally eclipse head and heart, in the process producing a pseudo clarity, accompanied by a pseudo feeling of flow. Two people may be so caught up in this mental and emotional storm that their "certainty" causes them to leave their marriages...often with disastrous results.

Our essential self doesn't want us to complicate our lives beyond the level of complexity that's necessary to lead a fulfilling existence. But sadly, while we were growing up few of us were taught the difference between insight and thoughts, feelings and emotional reactions. Consequently we tend to ignore the more logical and heartfelt aspect of ourselves when, tempted by a potentially destructive course of action, it asks, "Why should I?" Because it feels good is a poor excuse for doing something. Life should feel good, but it can only be truly good when we learn to approach every situation with our head and heart united, not based on wild emotions and conflicting thoughts. Otherwise there's a kickback.

If we allow thoughts to come and go without attaching ourselves to them, and simultaneously manage our emotional reactions by bringing our deeper feelings into the picture, we can save ourselves a heap of heartache. We can't rely on the voices in our head—the thoughts that come to us unbidden. Neither can we rely on our emotional impulses, driven as they are by chemistry and irrational thoughts. One is going to warn us to avoid a particular situation, whereas the other is going to say we might miss out on the best thing yet. In both cases the voice isn't our true head and heart, but that of our impulsive thoughts and emotions, both of which are features of our ego.

Becoming authentic is about learning to *use* your head instead of *losing* it.

Do you really want to live with interminable arguments with yourself? Do you want to subject yourself to an ongoing stew of emotional turmoil? Unless you are coming from head and heart, the name of the game will be confusion, anxiety, and *drama*.

Why were my businesses so successful? Because they were born from and nurtured by head and heart. My business acumen flowed from who I *am*. But when it came to relationships, I grew up lacking awareness of how head and heart work.

In business I didn't doubt my judgment. I approached everything from a state of "knowing." This is the pure clarity that arises when head and heart work in sync. Doubting ourselves, so that we are continually second-guessing ourselves, signals that we are being ruled by thoughts and emotions instead of real insight and true feeling.

I was *always* the entrepreneur because this gift of nature was nurtured in the circles in which I grew up. My heart was in it, with my head guiding me. At school in Belgium at the age of ten, I started selling chocolates. I'd buy them from the store next to the gas station and take them to school to market to students. The profit I made went into collecting miniature train sets. My father had the wit to discern and back this enterprising aspect of my authentic being, which was the chief part of me to survive childhood intact.

And the torment that swirled around my romance with my beloved living on a different continent? It was all because, in this area of my life, I was mistaking emotion for *feeling*, as well as mistaking thought for what my mind *knew*.

As clarity dawned, one question that kept cycling through my mind was whether my beloved would be able to love my boys. If the emotional bond between two people is strong, they may tend to override such issues, assuming that "love will find a way." Instead of telling myself, "If we really love each other," I chose to be absolutely honest with myself.

One aspect in particular troubled me—timing. I wanted

to go slowly, jumping to no conclusions but simply allowing things to unfold and flow as my clarity increased. I asked myself, "Does one of the most important decisions we can ever take need to be *that* urgent?"

The author and teacher Mark Nepo has some sound advice. "When feeling urgent," he writes, "you must slow down." He explains that the doorway to our next step of growth always lies *behind* the urgency we are feeling.

If a solid connection between mind and heart is either absent or deficient, we will struggle to make wise decisions. How many of us have rushed into situations out of our emotional need for "certainty," only to live to regret our haste?

If you find yourself going through a cost-versus-benefit analysis in a relationship, weighing plusses against minuses, the fact you're even thinking this way means you don't *yet* have the clarity required for a sound decision. This is when I believe it's time to slow down and honor what I have come to see as a four-step process that results in flow:

- Embrace the potential of what's occurring
- Examine the possible ways forward from a mindset of trust instead of fear.
- Engage challenges from a calm inner centeredness.
- Wait for clarity to emerge before you move into action.

Now that I was in the relationship, I felt it unwise to introduce my love to my boys until the two of us were clear that we intended to create a future together. They had experienced so much disruption. But how to be reasonably sure that the two of us did in fact have a strong chance of things working?

Because of my Islamic faith, I didn't feel it appropriate to live together before marriage. In my eyes you were either married or you weren't, with no middle ground. However, I was also seeing there was another side to this issue. Not having grown up in the same village as people used to back when so many of the rules I lived by were formulated, how could a man and woman from different parts of the globe spend time wanted and needed together to truly create a foundation for the future unless they spent time under the same roof? Traveling to and meeting in different countries simply wasn't the same as living together. Concluding that I was being old school and traditional, I thought, "Let's see how it feels to live together."

We were about to take the step I thought I could never take when a further complication arose. As we discussed our schedules for the months ahead, we discovered that my love had a commitment to be away the exact dates my two boys were due to spend time with me in Hong Kong. "That's great synchronicity," I commented.

"But what if I *wasn't* scheduled to be away?" she countered. "Would you kick me out during that time?" Given that things had lined up in such a way that we could avoid this dilemma, it was a hypothetical question. Yet for my love the issue was important and I needed to respect this.

Keeping in mind that when we pay attention to both head and heart, we don't omit practical matters in favor of a strong emotional pull, it was essential my new love ease into my boys' lives, giving them chance to welcome her. If practicalities are ignored, they will bite us in the butt.

I have witnessed how difficult it can be to blend families, even when it should be obvious to all parties that it's the right step to take. When a friend's wife died of a brain tumor, he was naturally concerned about who would raise their two children were something also to happen to him. He didn't consider his in-laws a viable option, so he married again, but on the condition they wouldn't have children. Then a freak occurrence upended his scheme. His new wife contracted a rare form of cancer that could only be reversed by the changes pregnancy causes in the body. The choice was either her death or add a child to the family. They chose to add a child. It took the mother a number of years to build trust with her husband's children from his former marriage. Now at last everybody treats her like their mother.

I had shown myself willing to change my entire approach to the issue of living together, but now the woman I loved asserted that before she moved in with me, she felt the boys *must* know we were in a relationship. We were at an impasse, with each of us expressing valid points of view.

I wanted to say yes to my love in consideration of what was important to her, while at the same time my deeper self knew that I really wanted to do the right thing for the boys. It wasn't a choice of head over heart, but involved allowing time for a clarity that's deeper than our fluctuating emotion to emerge—a "knowing" of what to do that's more profound than our often contradictory thoughts. Once such clarity arises, our intelligence and feelings sit side by side in equilibrium.

Until we reach such a balanced state, it's unwise to move forward.

I needed time, I realized. This was what I knew in my head and what I felt in my heart.

We had been due to spend ten days together at a magnificent health resort in Asia, during which I planned to begin writing this book. After more than seven years of incubating the insights I wanted to share, it had become clear to me that this was the moment to put pen to paper. This trip was therefore a landmark for me and one I wished to share with the woman I wanted to become my life partner. Instead, to honor where she was at that point in her journey, my love decided to spend Christmas with family in her own country.

A decision is right for the time it's made. Whether it will still be right tomorrow we can never know. We aren't asked to make decisions for tomorrow, only for today. Clarity can't be forced but has to emerge.

When we are present in each moment, life unfolds in its own flowing way. How do we know whether we are truly present? The answer is that when we are present, it isn't even a question. We don't even think about whether something is coming from head or heart. Because both are united, we simply know what action to take.

When we are no longer a stranger to ourselves—when we feel ourselves to be a part of the whole—connecting to another person isn't a matter of *trying to form* a connection, but of *becoming aware of the connection that already exists*. It's a recognition of what *is*.

As we embrace what's happening in our life, trustingly taking each step as it presents itself to us, clarity emerges. If we are to be connected to another in everyday life in some manner—whether in business, as friends, or romantically—the connection will become obvious as we "go with the flow."

No longer lonely but embracing this time of aloneness, I went to the resort, where I met with my editor and began writing this book. There was no doubt in my heart that I had made the appropriate choice, no second-guessing my decision. I would greatly miss my beloved's presence and think of her many times a day. However, I was clear about what my head and heart had in truth known all along. The relationship was indeed magical. But if we were to come together, the time was not to be now.

In every aspect of life, we need not only heart but also the mind with all its faculties switched on. This state of consciousness is far deeper than the kaleidoscope of empty-headed thoughts we all experience each day and so mistakenly refer to as our head. Our heart is our deepest feeling state, not our transitory and frequently turbulent emotions.

Make the mistake of mixing these up, as most do, and we invite chaos into our lives.

7

Who Comes First in Your Life?

Not just in romantic relationships but in all kinds of human relationships, people want to feel that they come "first" in the life of someone significant to them.

Friends feel slighted because the person they consider their best friend went to an event with a different person. A mother or father feel their daughter or son isn't paying them sufficient attention. Someone is upset because they weren't asked to be maid of honor or best man. People can even feel hurt because they weren't included in a dinner party or an office gathering.

Before I married the woman who became the mother of my children, I dated my father's partner's daughter. We intended to spend our lives together, until my father and his partner had a falling out. My intended was leaned on to persuade me to leave the negotiating table. She called me to tell me that if I continued at the table, I would in effect be choosing my father over her.

Given the nature of Asian families, this was a stunning

ultimatum. After contemplating its implications, I responded in the only way that felt appropriate: "It's sad, but you should probably choose your father and I will choose mine. But if we do that, years from now if you're not well, look to your left and to your right. See whether the people who convinced you to have this conversation are present."

We tend to underestimate the impact of such painful incidents, which we all experience in various forms.In the midst of this trauma, my father suffered a heart attack, which in retrospect seems symbolic. The break with his partner was truly heartbreaking. In 2004 I was diagnosed with cancer, and three years later my intended was also diagnosed with cancer.

Years later I discussed this traumatizing episode with my mother. "Do you realize that my intended and I have both been stricken with cancer?" I asked her. "Do you see any connection?" She didn't. I find that despite the scientific evidence of the effect of relationships on our health, none of those who had brought about our miserable situation appear to have connected the dots.

To this day I find it unbelievable that anybody could be so cruel as to impose such an ultimatum on their children, and yet it's often done in some parts of the world and some families. You are expected to put family first, whatever the price for your personal life.

In no relationship is this issue of who comes first more acute than in romantic relationships. In my own case, following my divorce, when it came to how I interacted with my beloved with respect to my two boys, she and I had a frank discussion of the issue of who comes first. People often look at love as if it were a pie with only so many pieces to go around. I prefer to think of it in terms of water. The same water found in waterfalls, streams, rivers, ponds, lakes, and vast oceans is also the water we pour into a glass to quench our thirst. Depending on the requirements of a particular circumstance, that's the shape the water takes.

Even as water is water, so also love is love. But it manifests differently according to what's required at the time. Each situation gets 100 percent of our love, just as a stream, a pond, or a lake are each 100 percent water. Its fluidity enables the form it takes to change. Love is infinite, not something restricted. It's ever flowing, not fixed like the pieces of a pie.

All of the categorizing of "how much" we love someone is of little importance and is simply ego marking its territory. What being with someone feels like in real-time is what has value. Labeling, evaluating, and critiquing are evidence of an inability to embrace a situation and trust, a lack that's nothing more than the ego's attempts to control the experience as a result of our insecurity.

I have come to see that the issue is never whether we are going to put one person ahead of another. Emotional reactivity and thoughts arguing back and forth will certainly construct such a conundrum. The whole idea of putting one or the other "first" is alien to real caring. To cast a situation in such an either-or light is a manifestation of the needy possessiveness associated with thought and emotion, not the wisdom characteristic of head or the caring that flows from heart.

When we set our ego aside, the idea of "first" has no relevance, since in every situation the question becomes one of *the priority at that particular moment*. In any situation, decisions need to be taken from a practical standpoint. If we allow either emotion or mental arguments to rule, we will betray both our head and our heart.

For a relationship to work, each of us needs to be at the center of our life, allowing everyone else to choose how they align themselves around us. We must be the sun in our solar system.

Does this sound like narcissism? On the contrary, it's when people aren't centered that they treat everyone and everything in a narcissistic manner, since an uncentered individual can't help but be needy—and consequently illogical and emotionally reactive.

When we are centered in a union of head and heart, others sense the contentment that accompanies embracing a situation, trusting, waiting for clarity, and moving forward in flow. Because we are solidly grounded, we have no need to control anyone. We exude a calm presence, which is immensely attractive to those whose lives deserve to be aligned with ours. The result is that, without our trying to arrange things, everybody spontaneously finds their place in our life, which corresponds to their own rhythm.

Real love isn't exclusive but inclusive. It doesn't ostracize, pushing people away. Rather, like water, it's capable of taking many different forms. Just because two people decide no longer to be together as a couple shouldn't end their love for each other. It should simply pass through a metamorphosis, like a chrysalis morphing into a butterfly that then becomes free to take off in a different direction. This allows us to include people in ways that are appropriate for life's many varied situations.

This is especially the case when someone new enters the picture. Many of us have a present beloved and also a former partner who continues to be part of our life. When someone comes new into a situation where there's a former partner, it can be challenging. How is it going to work? How are they going to react?

Years after my divorce, my entire family remains respectful of my former wife. Why? Because I'm respectful of her. The way I behave toward her influences how the rest of the family treat her. Since I welcome her with kindness, so also do my parents. Why would they do otherwise? To show such caring is nonnegotiable.

Bring a new partner into the picture and for many such an occasion becomes a nonstarter. It can plunge any conviviality into the toilet. Yet if people are differentiated—if they can simply be themselves, without imposing on others—why can't the new partner and the former spouse both be included? There's no box that says it has to be otherwise, other than an individual's ego. To embrace our situation and act from a mindset of trust dictates that this is the appropriate way to treat one another.

Whenever there's a former partner, there are bound to

be stories from your shared past to which your new partner doesn't directly relate, since she or he wasn't around at that time. There will be times when those stories are relevant and you want to be free to talk about them. Instead of this causing resentment or jealousy, it's important for the person who wasn't present to realize that without our past, neither of us would be who we are today.

When we look at someone's past not through the eyes of ego but in a way that values who they have become, experiences from the past become an asset instead of being seen as a deficit. Whereas one person's several breakups may show that they have learned nothing, another person may have learned how to be an ideal partner. In my own case, I came to see that my divorce wasn't something to kick myself over, but a situation to be embraced as a vital element of evolving into the person I am today.

At one point in a counseling session my wife said to me, "I am your biggest weakness. If you overcome this, you will be unstoppable." At the time, I wanted none of this. I'd rather keep the weakness than embrace the painful situation I was going through. What could embracing it possibly bring me, brownie points?

Prior to this critical juncture in my life, I walled myself off when I was in pain. Today if I'm in pain, I want to feel it. When we're in pain, we become poignantly aware of our mortality and the temporal nature of our life. However, allowing ourselves to feel our pain isn't at all the same as wallowing in it, which just feeds our anguish.

Whenever we find ourselves suffering, it's because we are fighting the pain, resisting it every step of the way—usually by telling ourselves stories about how "this shouldn't be happening." Embracing our situation and moving forward in trust radically alters the tenor of this experience. As we stop resisting, suffering melts into simply experiencing the pain. It may not be pleasant, but neither are we suffering.

In our next counseling session my wife simply said, "Please let me go." She had every freedom a spouse could ever want. In terms of how she spent her time, the opportunities available to her, as much money as she needed, the most incredible travel, and retreats with the world's foremost teachers, she had everything in abundance. Yet compared with being true to her feelings, she counted these things of little value. I at last realized that she needed to honor herself, trusting that she alone knew what was right for her. I had to honor the fact she felt trapped in a situation where she couldn't grow in the way she wished to.

We have to accept that it takes *two* to tango. The reality is that none of us has much influence over how another human being feels or whether they might decide to take a different direction during our years together. We have no control when it comes to what their particular needs may be.

Even with the wisest selection of a partner and expert preparation for marriage and children, there are no guarantees—and therefore there should be no shame, recrimination, or regret if a situation goes sideways. We take it all in our stride, adapting to each of the changes life thrusts upon us to stimulate our growth.

It's a matter of allowing our essential self to emerge and replace our need to control the course love happens to take. To give up trying to understand, let alone judging and attempting to control, is a vital step that can greatly reduce the negative impact of a breakup.

Life isn't predetermined. It plays out however it plays out, which is in many ways beyond our influence. There's no single "right way," and there are no certainties other than death, taxes, and change. In all of the confusion and chaos, there are however tremendous opportunities to shed ego and allow our authentic self, with head and heart united, to come to the fore.

8

Getting Clear About Clarity

66 I just didn't want to be near you," my former wife shared with me some time after our divorce. "I hated being around when you bulldozed to get what you wanted. Even when we were on vacation in some of the most beautiful spots on earth, you were an angry person."

I think back to a particular Wednesday when we were deciding where to go for dinner that Friday, our customary date night. It happened to be white truffle season, so I emailed the two concierge companies I used to get me a table, only to be informed there was no table available that particular Friday evening.

When I told my wife there wasn't a table, she countered, "You know we will be eating there on Friday. You want white truffles and so do I."

I was like, "What?"

To this she retorted, "Why are you wasting my time telling me we won't eat there, when we both know we will?"

Her words stopped me in my tracks as I asked myself,

What kind of monster am I?

Bulldozing certainly resulted in action, but no one felt happy doing what I had asked of them. No one can enjoy having to bow to a person who is throwing their weight around.

My story illustrates how different the ego is from our truly intelligent and deeply feeling authentic self. Today bulldozing is no longer a prominent feature of my approach to life, yet paradoxically I am now more powerful than ever, just as it was predicted I would be. Flow resulting from clarity has replaced bulldozing.

Once you realize you are acting from a bulldozing ego and not from your loving self, how do you change? Given that this behavior is deeply etched into our neural wiring, how do we rewire our brain to be in alignment with the authenticity that emanates from the union of head and heart?

Literally billions on the planet believe that the way to free ourselves from behavior that isn't representative of who we really are is to feel bad about ourselves, constantly apologizing and down on ourselves. Religions the world over have tended to take this approach to getting people to change. It's often referred to as "repentance."

Instead of leading to happy, productive lives that contribute lovingly and joyously to the advancement of the wellbeing of others, the result of such "repentance" in countless lives has been to generate a colossal burden of guilt and shame. This approach has failed abysmally to produce the loving, joyous, peaceful world we all hope for.

Now I want to share with you one of the most important

insights that has ever come to me. If you are down on your-self, expect to live a downer of a life. Being down on yourself will never bring about the kind of loving, caring behavior that springs only from being authentic. Can you guess why? It's because the only part of ourselves that's ever down on us is the ego. If you look closely, you'll see that the ego takes pride in how bad it has been!

The way to effect change in our dysfunctional neural patterns is revealed in the real meaning of the word repent, which isn't associated with the negative Latin origin of the English word promulgated by the churches. The Greek term simply means to change your mind by going through a meta-morphosis. This results in living in a manner that reflects your essential self instead of your ego.

Such a metamorphosis means we stop seeing ourselves as a worm or a screwup and instead embrace ourselves for the person we are. We trust in our essential goodness, which en-ables us to see ourselves in the clear light of day and results in behavior that flows from head and heart united.

When we make this switch, it impacts every aspect of our life. How? We no longer think of ourselves in the small-mind-ed way that causes the self-doubt that makes us feel we have to prove something and thereby triggers the misguided behav-ior of the ego.

All my years of feeling I wasn't good enough and relent-lessly driving myself to try to prove my worth served only to imprison me in the kind of behavior characteristic of the ego. Today I finally feel like I'm out of jail. I'm writing this book *because* I'm free of the need to impress anyone, including myself. I'm writing this book because, despite my success in business, for so many years I in many ways played small.

I want to be clear that transformation from smallness to greatness isn't a straightforward process. It doesn't happen lockstep and is, on the contrary, highly individualized. What it required for me to take this leap may be really different from what's needed in your case. However, I trust that my experience will illustrate how life orchestrates the transformation for each of us in a manner that's appropriate for us if we allow it to.

So many of our choices originate in a lack of awareness and are governed by factors of which we have no knowledge. To make truly informed choices from a state of clarity, where we really know what we are doing, requires us to develop a high level of awareness.

For example, I had a choice not to use my sharp tongue to say things that were hurtful in my marriage, but I lacked awareness of the impact of my words on those around me. It's for this reason that, when my oldest son remarked that his mother *had* to leave because she was with me, I was stunned. It was the coup de grâce to what my integrative doc had been telling me concerning my arrogance.

Once we become aware of how we have been driven by ego and begin to awaken to our authentic self, we cease being down on ourselves. In place of this deficit way of approaching things, life increasingly uses the people, situations, and change that are part of our everyday experience to open our eyes to the effect we have on others. To the degree that we're willing to become aware, we equip ourselves to challenge the ego-driven negative behavior of our false self.

The way to take up the mantle of responsibility for our actions is to align ourselves with our essential self, which lies beneath the habitual way of going about things characteristic of our ego. The more our choices originate from our clear center, not from how family and society programmed us, the more what we elect to do becomes the product of our own will. Only as life taught me to be willing to step back from my fixed ideas of who I was, observing and questioning my behavior until I had clarity, was I able to progressively take responsibility for my actions and finally become a free agent.

It's a question of showing up with absolute clarity in everything we do. We get clear about the unique requirements of each situation with which we are faced. Clarity is an asset I utilize constantly. As someone who knew me well remarked, "That's the difference between you and everybody else. You're clear it's going to happen, whereas they aren't." Once we're clear what needs to happen, we give it everything we've got—full effort for full return.

When I shifted away from bulldozing, I had to get the hang of how clarity works through flow, which is different from how it works through the bulldozing ego. Needless to say, just the right situations came along to school me. Given my love of white truffles, the truffle season once again figured in getting a little education along these lines.

I asked a client, "Would you like to have lunch?" I don't

function as well when my main meal is dinner, so for a business meal it's important that, as far as possible, it's over lunch. On this occasion I waffled and we ended up going to dinner. It was my invite, so I had no reason to compromise myself in this way. All the quality restaurants are aware that sometimes I decide to go out to eat at last minute and they have a way of keeping the odd table or two spare for just such occasions. Sometimes when its's last minute, I ask the restaurant personnel, "Do you think you might accommodate me for lunch, even if it's in the lounge?" Every time I've gone expecting to be in the lounge, there has been a table waiting for me in the main dining room. On this occasion, for the first time ever I didn't get a table. Why? Because my energy wasn't aligned, which meant my interaction with the restaurant team didn't receive my full intentionality.

It's amazing what's possible when you know how to go about things. You don't surrender your preferences, the things that really matter to you. Instead you *embrace* your preferences, which reflect your authentic being with its marvelous capacity to intend the very best for not only yourself but everyone concerned.

Let me show you how it works when we are in a state of flow. I had committed to a lunch and forgot I had done so. When I received a message that said *I'll meet you there*, I texted back to ask what the person was referring to. *We're supposed to have lunch in 15 minutes*, came the response. I set off walking and called the restaurant to see if they could help me out. No one is nutty enough to call a three-star Michelin restaurant 15 minutes ahead. Though they were really busy, they accommodated me. Why? Because I was fully aligned with what needed to happen.

You might think to yourself, "He's talking about intentionality." A lot of people stress the importance of intentionality. However, this can be a slippery term, in that it can refer to clarity and taking action on the one hand, while on the other hand it can refer to the tension generated by drivenness, which results in feeling we have to "make" something happen and bullying our way through the world. In my past, the tension and stress of living this way resulted in cancer and divorce. Today I leave all the tension out of the picture.

This isn't about simply setting your mind to do something. Lots of people set their mind to do something but then they get distracted or end up backing off, so that nothing happens. The reason is that their *being* isn't aligned with their mental intention. This is because they aren't clear. Intentionality without clarity is just fooling ourselves, whereas clarity without action lacks the power to achieve results. But the action needs to flow, not be forced.

To approach life in a state of flow, which is another word for wholeheartedness, is to allow our decision and our action the full expression they deserve. Such wholeheartedness springs from the state in which head and heart are united in an expression of authenticity. Without this, we have a tendency to keep our decisions and our actions somewhat apart, which many of us prefer because then we have an "out."

Countless people leave an opening. What they are really

doing is protecting themselves from disappointment in case what they want doesn't materialize. To tell themselves they are protecting themselves is a lack of trust and therefore risks denying them what they want, since believing in the possibility that something *won't* happen means they create space for it *not* to happen.

It also means they aren't going to take the steps that are needed to ensure it happens. Consequently they don't get the appointment, don't get the room, don't get the table at the restaurant. If you know what's got to happen, you don't leave openings like that. The matter becomes nonnegotiable.

A wise monk used to say that faced with any decision, we like to leave a part of ourselves out of the equation. We commit to things, except that we like to be sure there's an escape clause. Describing us as "inveterate two-timers," he went on to explain that we absolutely dread the thought of the whole of our being coming together in a "yes" to somebody or something, with nothing of ourselves left out and therefore no possibility of retreat. In other words, we secretly fear basing our actions on head and heart united, unaccustomed to functioning this way as we are.

To bring my whole self to everything I do, which is the state of flow, is a key factor in my work. I think of the time when a child with severe allergies was in crisis. Since my team were finding it difficult to obtain an appointment with the top allergist, I decided to assist. "I understand your'e extremely busy and have no openings," I told the allergist's reception desk. "I know you're doing your best. But imagine this was your son. Imagine yourself as his mother. Are you going to be able to function effectively, let alone sleep soundly, as long as your son is suffering in this way? Well, that's what we're dealing with—a child who is suffering and a mother who feels helpless. I just know I can count on you to see whether there is some way to open up an appointment." Fifteen minutes later I received a phone call and the appointment was confirmed.

Let me reiterate that this isn't about bulldozing and neither is it about begging, both of which involve ego. It's all about the powerful energy of flow that arises spontaneously when head and heart are united. Nothing about me was either bullying or begging. It was simply a matter of following through on the clarity that had come to me.

We first have to be crystal clear. We know something is the right thing, which is why we believe in it. We trust the direction we are taking. Flow then carries us forward, spontaneously providing both the determination and the wisdom we require to achieve the result we seek. You might say that clarity and flow are two sides of a single coin.

There are numerous aspects of ourselves we can rewire once we begin to be aware—aspects that will make all the difference to the quality of our own life as well as the lives of others. This is what the religious term repentance is about— upping the quality of our life because we at last embrace who we are, believe in ourselves, trust our judgment, are clear about our direction, and flow all but effortlessly in the direction we need to go.

Instead of trying to change by being down on ourselves, all we are asked to do is become aware of our real self in each and every situation. The opposite of being made to feel small, you might say it's finding our equivalent of the authentic "Bagger Vance swing." You saw the movie Bagger Vance, starring Will Smith and Matt Damon, didn't you?

The movie depicts a case of "him against himself." This is the predicament we all find ourselves in—our ego against simply being our real self. There was a swing that was coming from Bagger as he had grown up thinking of himself, and there was a swing that emanated from his true self, which had become largely buried in childhood. He needed to find his authentic swing, which was an expression of the flow that originated in his core *being*. To achieve this, he had to search deep within himself for the golfer he was born to be, then embrace this more authentic aspect of himself and trust that it would take him where he was born to go.

To evolve in this way is to experience true metamorphosis.

9

Transform Your Deficits into Assets

As we shed our ego and become increasingly authentic, we aren't asked to give up a single thing that's true to who we are. This is why I don't like to use the term surrender. Instead, each element of our real self gets drawn into the spotlight, where it can be developed and finally revealed in all its magnificence. We step out of our smallness into our greatness.

In my case, I've brought all my skills with me into my new life, minus the need to prove anything. The clarity, confidence, and trust in life that I once used in an unhealthy manner are now all employed in ways that appeal to people's basic humanity. With my ego and its bulldozing ways largely in check, my ability to spot possibilities and bring them to fruition has intensified. It's the far more relaxed mindset I'm coming from and the energy of flow I show up with that's different.

My current work brings me into proximity with many

sick people and their physicians, and sometimes this involves members of my own family. On one occasion my mother needed surgery, so we attended an appointment with the surgeon. While we were paying for the visit and finalizing arrangements for the hospital stay, the nurse at the desk asked my mother, "Are you on any medications?"

"I take aspirin," my mother answered. Her response caught both the nurse and myself by surprise. Since aspirin is a blood thinner, it necessitated a rescheduling of the surgery so that the aspirin was completely out of her system, which meant waiting a further five days.

Even though the hospital has 50 floors, the nurse was unable to schedule a room for five days' time. So I waited a couple of days, then called the desk. Although it's not a hospital I generally use and their approach is different from mine on many issues, they have the best equipment for the kind of surgery my mother needed, so I was determined to find her a bed. The desk said they would see what they could do.

It's always been my nature to think outside the box. Now that I'm no longer trying to prove my worth, I find all the more that I don't see boxes. With nothing to prove to anybody including myself, I enjoy total freedom to pursue whatever action constitutes the right move for a given situation. By simply seeking the best way forward, I'm free to do what others could never imagine themselves doing.

The next morning I dropped my boys off at school, then went to the hospital in person. The nurse recognized me because she used to work at another hospital where I'm well known. "How are you?" I asked.

"What are you doing here?" she inquired.

"I called yesterday to ask for a bed for my mother. You said you'd look into it. I'm here to finalize arrangements for her room."

"But you only called yesterday," she said.

"I know it was yesterday, but this is urgent. I'm going to sit over there and wait while you allocate my mother's room." I made sure I didn't sound at all annoyed, just matter of fact with a friendly tone.

"What do you mean?" she pressed.

"I'll just wait," I affirmed.

Although I could see from the look on her face that she was telling herself, *This guy is crazy,* an hour later I had a bed for my mother. What made it happen? Quite simply my clarity that it was what needed to happen. To ensure my mother was assigned the hospital bed she needed, I simply showed up and remained present.

My external action was a reflection of my inner state of clarity and was an expression of flow. Instead of repeatedly calling and by so doing becoming both annoying and frustrated, which is the opposite of flow, I brought my full self to the situation, which involved parking my carcass opposite the reception. It didn't matter that the nurse receptionist thought I was nuts. I wasn't aggressive in any way, just a powerful *presence.*

When we're in flow, we are intensely present. This is why flow is a state someone can't ignore. I had left the nurse no opening for anything other than to do her best in response to my best effort on behalf of my mother. What matters is that ultimately she did what was being asked of her because she was inspired by my wholehearted dedication to my mother's wellbeing, not because I was intimidating her. My Bagger Vance had emerged. Feeling my clarity, seeing my commitment, she genuinely wanted my mother to have a bed.

A woman who works with J. P. Morgan remarked following a workshop, "We were all sitting waiting for the workshop to begin when you walked in. You didn't say a word, but it was very clear you had arrived."

I asked her, "What do you mean?"

"We could *feel* you," she explained. "You just came in and sat down, but everybody knew you had arrived." This is the kind of presence we exude when we are in flow.

Becoming self-aware, or what's often referred to as "enlightened," doesn't take our talents and skills away, it simply changes the way we approach life so that our deficits are transformed into assets. It changes our mindset and therefore at times our methods. To understand how to move people in a way that isn't coming from ego but capitalizes on our ability to lead them from a state of flow is vital.

This is the approach I now use in virtually all aspects of my everyday activities. It's about learning to embrace life's way of sending us just the right people and situations to facilitate our metamorphosis. Instead of being angry when things don't go my way, I now embrace everything as a blessing... and look for the opportunity it contains.

I find every moment of life to be one in which I want to be fully present so that I not only experience it fully but catch the opportunities as they occur. Recall what Toscanini's son said about his father: "Whatever he happens to be doing at the moment is the biggest thing in his life—whether it is conducting a symphony or peeling an orange."

"Everything is important to you," I've had people say to me.

Do you know what? They're right. When you are fully present, each moment is just as important as the next. So there is indeed a sense in which everything is indeed important to me.

Perhaps you can understand why, in response to people saying that everything is important to me, I often ask, "So nothing is important to you, or very little?"

The hospital room for my mother was important. The appointment for the child with the allergist was important. But so also is the choice of restaurant.

You might counter that a restaurant isn't a matter of life and death, and yet in a way it is. It's a question of really *living* life, instead of dragging ourselves corpse-like through the motions, barely getting by, so that our time here on earth is pretty much mundane and our experiences mostly mediocre.

To live in flow means that whatever may be occurring in *this* moment is important. If it's on your front burner, it's important. What was important yesterday or an hour ago was important then. The important thing right now is what's presenting itself right now.

The reason I so deeply embrace all I undertake is that the way I approach something like a CT scan is the way I approach everything else. In fact I have come to see that this is an important aspect of embracing life. When you embrace life, you stop categorizing things as important or unimportant. You plunge into each of your experiences with your whole being.

If you think about it, categorizing in the way people do involves a measure of rejection, a "saying no" to certain things instead of a full-on participation in each moment. It's a refusal to really *live* during large chunks of our time here.

I find that when I completely embrace each situation as it arises, treating it as if it's just right for that particular moment, I have so much gratitude for each aspect of my journey that I approach everything with the same keen awareness and commitment. No moment, whatever it may contain, is less important than any other—no moment to be rejected by being rated "lesser than."

If you want to go to a particular restaurant, you do what everybody else considers it not worth bothering to do. If you know the restaurant personnel well, you email. If you don't, you call. Whether you get the table can still depend on a variety of factors. However, when you put forth the maximum effort you are capable of in that moment, you can accept the outcome without feeling disappointed if it's not what you hoped for. Not every time, but nine times out of ten, you're going to be delighted with the outcome.

You might wonder, "But what if everyone took the same

approach? The whole world can't eat at the best restaurants, seated at the best table." My answer is simple. As more and more of us wake up to what really living involves, mediocre service, mediocre food, and mediocre decor will become a thing of the past. When the demand is there, we will all up our game, because the resources on this planet are plentiful.

Mediocrity represents a failure to fully embrace life, a failure to trust in life's goodness and our own potential for good, a complete lack of clarity about what's important, and zero flow. But as long as we're willing to tolerate mediocrity, that's what we'll get.

It beggars belief what people are willing to put up with. Years ago in Burundi, fighting was taking place across the border between the Hutu and Tutsi. I was in a restaurant in Bujumbura when rockets began flying back and forth. We had a factory in Bujumbura and were distributing anti-HIV drugs and generic pharmaceuticals. I asked my partner, "How far are we from the front?"

"Twelve, maybe fifteen kilometers," he said.

I pressed, "You're sure they aren't going to hit us, right? Because I'm not really in the mood to get blown up."

"Don't worry about it," he said, essentially dismissing what was occurring as if it were normality. So we kept eating. *Bon appétit.*

In society as it is presently, people are trained to stay below the radar. They are taught to play dead by compromising themselves, selling themselves out, not standing up for what matters to them. They learn to skate on the surface of everyday life without ever experiencing the flow attached to being truly present.

A great deal of what goes under the rubric of "spirituality" is really a means of justifying mediocrity and the lack of presence it embodies. Authentic spirituality is about making the most of each and every moment, each and every situation, so that we enjoy life to our maximum capacity. How sad that most spiritual paths focus on *tolerating* rather than on embracing and *celebrating*.

Hopefully one day the level of awareness on our planet will reach a tipping point and everybody will begin to ask, Is it worth being like this? Why can't it be otherwise? Does there have to be so much mistrust? Why all this anger and hatred?

When you are accustomed to enjoying the best, you want this for others. You want it for the entire planet. Your life becomes dedicated to making a difference in each and every situation, small or large, local or global. Writing this book is an aspect of what I'm doing to try to help people see the ridiculousness of the way our world functions. I want to help awaken people, help them become aware, so that the entire world can live in flow, with all the benefits it brings. My aim is for the extraordinary to become a habit that replaces tolerating the intolerable.

So much becomes possible when we are real and connect meaningfully in the moment, then use our assets to improve a situation. All that's required for this to happen is to actually *be* where we are and to be truly *with* the people we're with. This is what embracing a situation means. We show up wholeheartedly and do our best in the situation.

When we embrace a situation with both head and heart, move forward with trust instead of fear or negativity, and take the time to become clear what needs to happen, it's amazing what a difference the flow we experience can make.

10

The Tea Boy

―――――――

"Business is business." How often have we heard people make such a statement? Most of the time we just buy into it, unaware of how utterly illogical and ultimately false this way of thinking is. To buy into this is to stab yourself in the foot.

One of the key aspects of life in which many of us fail to fully embrace our situation is our work. People go to jobs they dislike, while employers create workplaces that do nothing to engender a love of the work their team are engaged in. With a mentality of "business is business," how can we expect people to be engaged in what they do?

Trust is another vital element of good business. It's important to us that everyone we engage with from the supply chain to the customer trusts us and knows that our products are going to meet their expectations. It's for this reason that, in my companies, service is at the heart of everything we undertake. From the top down, everyone is dedicated to service—and as CEO it's my job to model the company's ethic.

People say to me, "The salesperson is supposed to perform the service, not you. You're supposed to run the corporation."

I respond, "If all we accomplish is to move inventory from our warehouse to the distributor's warehouse, what have we achieved?" I explain that we've essentially shoved a product down their throat that they can't sell. Then I explain, "But if we move product from our warehouse to the distributor's warehouse, then the distributor moves it to a satisfied customer who doesn't feel like they are being taken for a ride, now we've achieved something. That's *real* business."

When we do the right thing, it always makes business sense because *we* are being real, which involves head *and* heart. This is the only way of doing business that makes sense, since if we sell something to someone and it's not truly in their best interest, it will backfire. Not only will they not come back to us, but everyone networks—family, friends, and the organizations to which they belong. Are they going to be badmouthing us or singing our praises?

Many seem interested in making money in the short term, flooding the market with shoddy products and poor services with no view to sustainability. We've seen example after example of individuals who get the top position but have no love of the product and end up driving the company into the ground, only to be rewarded with an obscenely large golden parachute. Such individuals have never embraced their work. Their only real skill was misleading people, which is the opposite of building trust. Their love was the money, the image, the power, not being of service. It's why in time even the biggest names disappear from the high street, the mall, and the stock market.

When we say something like "business is business," it's a cop-out for not being in integrity—a cover for our dishonesty. We're excusing ourselves for not doing the right thing by the customer. Instead of being *real* with the people we're supposed to be serving, we're coming from the falsity of ego.

This is the kind of reasoning we engage in when we buy into our thoughts, not our wisdom, and are detached from our heart. No head, no heart—and authenticity nowhere in sight.

Life works best in every dimension when we step out of hiding, are real, and simply do whatever is appropriate at any given moment, using head and heart to give our utmost. A person who embraces their business activity, believes in themselves, gains clarity on an issue, and trusts life doesn't have time to waste on phoniness. We don't hide behind roles, facades, rank, or image.

Sometimes when people don't know who I am, they'll ask and I say, "I'm the tea boy."

"No way," they say.

I explain, "I bring the tea and I run the company. What's the difference?"

I have no issue serving tea to my team because it's all a continuum in which we share our particular talents with one another, serving in whatever way we can for the good of the whole. If tea is needed while my people are working intensively on a project, and I'm free to brew and pour it, that's what I do. That's what any good CEO should be doing.

I was talking to a friend about Gary Chapman's book *The 5 Love Languages*. One of these languages focuses on acts of service. I find that it's second nature for me to try to make even the service offered by top concierge companies appear like a kindergartener's attempt at service. In the business world, genuine service has tremendous value. While service is something we today see less and less, some of the emerging nations in the East are becoming adept at it.

When you forget about serving the customer, you've lost your way. Sadly most organizations don't look at their product as a means of serving. They buy with a philosophy that's focused on the cheapest they can obtain the product and the most they can sell it for and get away with it. The way I look at it is the exact opposite. Our mission statement is to provide quality products at an affordable price so that we balance profit, quality, and affordability, and really do everything in our capacity to make this equation work. When you are authentic, head and heart inform everything you do.

In today's market, many companies say, "Launch—then tweak, tweak, tweak." This is nothing more than putting themselves first. It doesn't come from authenticity, putting a product out to really help people, but from the "business is business" mentality that's all about making a buck. You know you are going to considerably inconvenience the people you are selling to, but you still put the product out there before it's ready.

I'm from the old school. We don't launch until we get it right. Yes, we miss out on opportunities, but we also avoid the bumps. It's a matter of only launching a product that's good, which is what people who are being real do, because a relaunch is twice as difficult if you mess up the first time. Why would people trust you again? I'd rather be late, get it right, and build trust than be early and inconvenience our customers. I don't expect the consumer to be forgiving, which is what so many companies count on. I want people to trust us from the get-go.

I joke with my competitors, "When you sell a product, you should deliver a box of aspirin with it, because you're guaranteed to produce a headache."

I want to know which product is the best quality and how I can buy it in such a way as to make it affordable. For instance, I was buying notebooks for back to school. Some of my competitors were selling notebooks with paper weighing 50-55 grams, whereas I was selling notebooks with paper that weighed 70 grams. Why? Because when you write on the heavier weight, it doesn't go through to the other side. With the competitor's product, you can see your writing on the reverse side, which means you're really getting a single-sided page instead of double-sided.

In one situation in which we were the number two supplier, several new competitors entered the market. Since we were preparing for the next season and my team were freaking out, I asked them, "What do you think we should do?"

"We should cut our price," they said.

"How exactly are we going to do that?" I pressed.

"We'll either have to negotiate the buying price down still lower or cut the quality," they all agreed. In other words, instead of going with 70 gram paper, we would drop down to 60 grams, just above the competitors' 50-55 grams.

Bringing both head and heart to bear on the situation, I did the opposite. I improved the quality of the notebooks, so that the gap between the competitors and ourselves was even greater. To achieve this, I negotiated like I'd never negotiated in my life. The result was that we were selling a product that had zero competition, while maintaining our profit margin.

This is why it's crucial to be authentic, with both head and heart fully engaged as we pursue our business. When we are authentic, we don't compromise our integrity. We see the bigger picture in which *business is a reciprocal exchange between human beings who all need to make a living, all have a need for certain goods, and all deserve to be treated as we would treat ourselves.*

Caring and serving others become the foundation for everything we do. It's crucial to show true caring at every touchpoint of our lives. Authentic caring is totally different from a facade of caring. What makes the difference? Anything less than a full-on effort to serve to the best of our ability originates from worrying about how we are being perceived instead of just being true to ourselves.

This is a manifestation of a *lack of self-worth*. There is an absence of trust, coupled with a failure to really embrace what we are engaged in. Because we don't truly believe in ourselves, we don't fully believe in the products we bring to market or the service we provide.

When we have something to prove, *it's because what we are doing doesn't speak for itself.*

Doing our best by showing up fully is all that's required because, after all, how can we ever do more than this? We can't be today where we might be tomorrow. This makes sense of Maya Angelou's comment that when she *knew* better, she *did* better. She was pointing to the vital element of clarity. We can only perform to the limits of what we know right now, what we are clear about. As soon as we have more insight, we are in a position to go further—but not until.

Trying to excel in order to prove something to yourself or others will actually mar your efforts because it isn't authentic. If you are motivated by trying to prove something, you'll produce less than your best, since such a mindset will both zap your imagination and sap your energy. You'll be far less creative than you are capable of being were you in the state of flow.

All we need is to know deep in our being that, based on our present level of awareness—our degree of consciousness at *this* particular point in our journey—we're fully engaged, embracing our situation, and therefore doing the best we can.

A young lady asked me, "How can I know when I've done my best?"

I answered, "If you pay attention to what you are truly feeling, you will know when you are functioning at your full capacity in a given moment. If you are honest with yourself and engage the process, it will be obvious."

When we are in flow and therefore doing our best, second-guessing ourselves, as so many of us do, doesn't even enter the picture because it isn't helpful and stems from self-doubt. In fact, dwelling on what we "could have" done is disruptive of flow. I don't want my team to tell me what they "could have" done, which simply manifests a failure to fully embrace a project at the time they needed to take action.

I'm not suggesting that connections aren't sometimes bumpy. I'm not saying that every conversation is going to go smoothly. If things are bumpy, then I work with them to obtain the best outcome possible in light of the difficulty. We are all a work in progress, which means we are going to hit some speed bumps.

When you've done everything you can and things still don't feel right, the enlightened approach is to enjoy the situation anyway. If I have a sense that I should do something because it's arising from the stillness of being, I've learned that I should do it no matter the hurdles and downsides. This is what embracing a situation entails, and it's an important aspect of living in a state of presence and flow. Life doesn't always give us a smooth ride, but we can nevertheless always have a valuable experience.

In terms of your work or activities, the point is to be happy with what you are accomplishing instead of anxious about what something might say about you. When you are in flow, you don't worry about what something says about you. You are simply being real in each moment. When this is your approach, what you do confirms your sense that you are valid. Because your contribution is authentic, it can't help but be valuable.

No matter what aspect of life we are talking about, I want to provide people with a reason to give their best. Whether this concerns an employee, a waiter, or someone furnishing me with a product I wish to purchase. I treat them in a way that evokes in them the desire to perform to their capacity— an embracing of what they are doing. Their best may not look the same as my best, but that's not the issue. All that matters is that they are doing their best, and I appreciate it. They feel my gratitude, which in turn inspires them to excel not as a matter of ego, but because they enjoy being the person they are.

In business this means being so well versed with what's involved that head and heart function in unity. Intelligence and deep feeling are part and parcel of each other. There's no division between what the head and the heart want, and no compartmentalizing of our lives.

There can be no scamming, no shoddy work, no half-hearted effort when we are being true to ourselves. Our authenticity generates a state of being that allows the *full-on power of flow* to exert itself as it guides us moment by moment.

11

Are You Empowering People or Fostering Dependence?

There's a freedom in not being dependent. I believe that at heart we all want this freedom. We want to take charge of our life, be an entrepreneur, be our own boss, or work with a team in a manner that allows our skills to be drawn out.

The problem is that because of the way many of us have grown up, we possess neither the determination nor the discipline. Not only have we never actually been empowered, our initiative was actively squelched from a young age. Consequently few of us seem to have any real understanding of our capacity.

Unless we challenge ourselves to go as far as we can, we can't possibly know what our capabilities are. This is why change comes into our life. My experience is that what I can achieve changes based on how far I'm willing to let life's challenges stretch me. An important aspect of empowering people is to encourage them to allow the things that occur in their lives to stretch them instead of resisting.

If you don't allow yourself to be stretched, how do you know what you are capable of? If you never take a risk, never bet on yourself, how do you know whether something is possible for you? Unless you try something, or at least look into it, how can you know whether you will like it? Whether it's food, a business venture, a relationship, an activity, or a spiritual practice, you can only know whether it's for you by exploring it.

In a situation in which there was some disagreement as to the way forward, a friend did what people who pride themselves on being "spiritual" say you should do, which is to meet someone where they are. I challenged this approach. What if the individual is in a place that's unproductive?

If we are to empower people, it's crucial to strike a balance between meeting them where they are versus nudging them forward, without of course bulldozing or dragging them. There's a need to be respectful by creating a safe space so that the person knows they aren't being judged.

We also need to be clear that there are times to lead. People benefit from a combination of being met and being led, not just met. We help them by respecting where they are, yes. At the same time, it's important not to give up on opening their eyes to a challenging situation's possibilities, though free of any kind of imposition.

This balance is especially important in the case of those in the helping professions, such as psychotherapists, counselors, social workers, personal coaches, and the clergy. Many who serve in one of these capacities view themselves as only there to listen. They listen, and listen, and listen. When they only listen, they introduce enormous openings for resistance, fostering unlimited opportunity for the person to wallow in their issues.

When we do this, we're not helping because the person ends up not moving. In truth we betray what our profession is all about. As an effective counselor one must meet individuals then lead them. We must do so in a manner that helps the individual embrace their situation, trust that what's occurring can benefit them, and arrive at a place of clarity—all while avoiding *ever* telling them what they should do.

People find themselves becoming empowered when we are there to ask precisely those questions that can trigger the reflection and introspection required for clarity to emerge from beneath their jumbled thoughts and tangled emotions. The individual then brings about the desired shift for themselves.

It's for this reason that if someone asks me a question, I invariably answer with a question. If my team members come to me with a question, I rarely give them the answer. I want the answer to be something they come up with. I find that individuals own the solution when it comes out of their mouth. When they are allowed to make the leap for themselves, I usually find that about 95 percent of the answer they come up with derives from engaging the question. Framing our questions in a manner that's likely to evoke an insightful response is therefore crucial.

Any change we want to see in a person needs to come

from within the individual themselves if it's to gain real traction. It's a matter of awakening a person's innate desire to exercise independence, which is how we each find within ourselves the discipline to do the things we need to do. Once someone learns to practice self-discipline, it's my experience that they revel in it. They take pride in their ability to show up at the appointed hour, fulfill tasks on schedule, pay their bills on time, keep their closet neat and their living space tidy, and maintain an orderly workspace. And let me be clear that I'm not talking about what's generally referred to as "type A" drivenness.

Whether you are a parent, a professional coach of some sort, a doctor, or a member of the clergy of one spiritual path or another, the key is to empower people versus fostering dependency. You help them shift into a mindset in which problem solving is second nature. Rather than acting as a crutch, you draw out their creativity, help them explore their talents, and encourage them to develop resilience.

I believe we have a responsibility to help individuals see how they can fulfill themselves through being true to themselves and simultaneously allowing who they are to impact others. However, as soon as I make such a statement, I hear you telling yourself, "But it's not my job. It's not my place to interfere in people's lives. They all have their own journey to take, their own path to walk."

A line in the movie *Woodlawn* says, "You give hope for what's possible." I see it as my duty as a fellow human being to share hope. As someone who recognizes how we all need each other if we are ever to reach for our potential as a species, I'm compelled to do so. I don't nudge people out of arrogance, but out of being real with them. I do so not only because giving them hope is the right thing to do, but *because it's possible.*

If we have been blessed with experience, understanding, and wisdom, we need to be aware that meeting someone where they are without either nudging or leading does nothing to benefit them.

You might argue, "Where's the respect you mentioned for where they are as a person?" What if where someone is as a person is fuzzy, lacking all clarity? What if life has so screwed them up that they can't see straight? What if they are so self-absorbed with the pain they are in that they have no hope of escape unless someone pulls them out of the quicksand that's swallowing them alive?

I feel that many people haven't been given the opportunities that could make all the difference, so my philosophy is, "Give someone the opportunity to be good, because other people haven't given them that opportunity. Create an opportunity for everyone, because at heart everybody is good." It's a matter of identifying the appropriate way for people to access their center and express themselves. I see it as my responsibility to help create opportunities for this to happen.

The term "create" is such an important one. Don't leave things to chance. We already touched on what tends to happen when we leave things to chance. This is why our world is in such a mess. It's my responsibility to do something about the state of things, and it's yours also. So why not spend the time we have here on this planet together to help those who have lost their way by nudging them and showing them a little of what's possible?

Instead of throwing up all the conceivable objections to taking action, my boys always say, "Why not?" Due to the way they were brought up, it doesn't work for me to dish out the *Because I said so* to which I hear so many parents resort. That's to treat them as inferior, as if they weren't really people. It's to weaken them, fostering dependence instead of empowering.

Instead I realize they have a point. If it's possible, why not? Why are so many of us always so against this or that? Why can't we be *for* more things? If you *can* do something that will help someone, then why on earth wouldn't you? If it's possible, why not make it happen? Isn't this what to truly embrace someone implies?

I have been privileged to enjoy a wealth of experiences few do more than dream of. It means I've learned a few things and have a few gems to share. Like me, you too have much to share. The trick is not to do it from a pulpit. Nudging isn't at all the same as preaching to a person or riding their ass.

An important aspect of empowering people involves a willingness to delegate, which requires selecting the right individuals to take on each particular task. Once we make the selection, we are required to trust them enough to cut them loose to perform the assignment.

My head buyer and I had been buying all the goods for

Angola together for five years. Each week we went over everything that came in and everything that was sold. In those months when I was in the office and not traveling or on vacation, we reviewed our situation together. This head buyer witnessed how 95% of the buying was so on target that our inventory required only minor tweaking every week or two. Eventually I said to her, "From now on, you do the buying. Treat me as someone who's just along for the ride." Her key performance indicator, referred to in the trade as a person's KPI, required her to ensure we were never either out of stock or overstocked.

To give someone this level of control in a business involving millions of dollars, you have to have confidence in your judgment that you selected the appropriate person. Once you have an effective system of checks and balances in place, you need to be willing to let go. This requires a centeredness and calmness, which allows you to trust.

Empowering others means you accept that no one is going to be you, but that if you allow them to take the reins, they will achieve perhaps 90 or 95 percent of what you might achieve. And who knows? They may even exceed you. The point is that to trust in this way frees you to focus on where you can add the most value.

Trust isn't blind, but informed.

Jump forward a few years. After my wife decided she and I no longer belonged together and I was about to launch Qineticare, I went on a silent retreat. When I returned to the office, it was to one of the worst inventory positions we had ever encountered. I didn't react, just calmly observed. One week went by, then two. My team came to me and asked, "Don't you care about Angola anymore? Is your only concern Qineticare?"

I responded, "Since you think I don't care, ask me any question about the inventory or about the business in general." Question followed question, and they were amazed to find that I knew exactly what was happening on every front. They wanted to know what I was doing these days, so I told them, "Watching."

"Watching what?"

"Watching you, seeing what you're going to do about our inventory issue. Based on that, I'll decide what I'm going to do."

"When will that be?"

"When I feel I've watched you sufficiently."

This approach is how I exercise trust. They naturally thought I was nuts. What if my strategy didn't work? "Worst scenario, I'll fix it when I'm on the ground," I assured them with full faith in myself.

"But you spend only one day per city, so how are you going to pull that off?"

That whole year, I stepped back in trust...and they stepped up. The profitability of the company increased by 50 percent. Using their skill sets, they took the game to another level and actually outperformed me. "My goal is to see how I can earn more by working less," I kept telling them. "I want to be the laziest guy on earth." Of course, they knew this was bull. But the point was that when we step back in the right way and people are forced to rely on their own initiative, everyone steps up.

I need to be clear that they weren't working longer hours. They were simply making decisions they never had to make before, which gave those with abilities superior to mine in certain areas the opportunity to shine. Some were better at paying attention to detail, others more focused. They may not have been able to see what was around the corner, but that was my responsibility. It takes a certain mastery of your craft to spot what lies ahead before anybody else does.

I think of people as consisting of three different types. The first group, life gives them a gentle push and they wake up to themselves and their situation's possibilities.

Some of my people possess real genius. I say they possess it, but it's a developed skill. You can read all the books on neuroplasticity and genius, and you may even have certain genetic advantages, but the genius comes through hard work and continuously being out of your comfort zone. My team learned from observing me in action.

The second group, life kicks them in the ass and they wake up. Being in business has been a learning process not only for myself, but for all with whom I'm connected. To trust to the point that we allow one another to learn the lessons we need to learn is essential.

My team also learned from watching some of our key people learn lessons. Time and again I watched team members and my partners make moves I knew weren't in our best interest. I would share with them my perspective, but then I had to trust them to do what they felt was right.

When things didn't turn out as they expected, I said nothing, which was crucial. In business you have to learn not to cry over spilt milk. Once you begin crying over spilt milk, it's the beginning of the end.

One of my partners persuaded me that we should invest in a country from which we ultimately had to walk away. Although he was keen on the investment, I never was. I shared my reservation. Since he was confident, I backed him anyway. I had a knowing, but I needed to let him go through what he needed to go through. It involved a half-million dollars, which was a lot of money for us at the time. Ten years later sitting on a plane together, he confessed, "I felt horrible when we first lost the money and you said nothing."

"What would have been the point of adding salt to the wound?" I responded. We had both been taught that we should never cry over spilt milk, but it's easier said than done. We may understand it conceptually, but to put it into practice can be challenging.

"The perspective I gained from that incident was unprecedented," he said. He was right. We ended up making many times more per annum on a consistent basis. The lesson learned brings the blessings, for it allows people to show up for the talented leaders they are. Such individuals also learn the value of allowing themselves to be stretched to the point of discomfort.

The third group are different. Life practically has to break their legs, screaming at them, "If you don't wake up and smell the coffee, I'm going to bury your ass."

To illustrate, one year millions of dollars of Christmas goods arrived in Angola, but my team on the ground for some reason seemed unable to clear it and get it out into the stores. We're talking about fridges, freezers, washing machines—the sort of goods people look forward to buying during the holiday period. It was therefore imperative that arrangements be made for clearing the cargo the moment it arrived. What good would millions of dollars of Christmas merchandise be in January?

A month before the Christmas season, when I realized we were in a crunch, I contacted my CFO to see what he was doing about the matter. He repeatedly affirmed that he was following up on it. Each time I called, I received the same assurance.

When January came around, my team were visibly upset. "Do you know what kind of a beating we're going to take from port charges?" they asked.

"Yeah, I know," I told them. "Right now we're at $240,000. By the time I take action, it'll be at $300,000 and change."

"We're talking US dollars," they exclaimed.

"I'm aware of that," I said.

"So why don't you do something *now?*" they pressed.

They knew me as Mr. Fix-it, who always did whatever I had to do. But this time I said quite calmly, "No, I'm going to continue watching for a while."

When ego is in charge, we are bound to be anxious. At times we'll even panic. It's important to keep in mind that ego majors in fear, which is the opposite of trust. Our authentic self in contrast is calm and trusting. Even when the heat is on and everything is at risk, we calmly assess the situation and take any action required without going into emotional overdrive or painting all kinds of frightening scenarios in our thoughts. We can remain calm because when we are being authentic, we have nothing to prove to anyone, including ourselves.

While I can be Mr Fix-it when required, my calm trusting approach also allows me to watch members of my team as they get into train wrecks. On such occasions, I watch without intervening—or at least not intervening too early. While these crashes may initially appear disastrous, I've learned that, managed well, they can take a company to a higher level.

When I again called my CFO, he persisted with the approach he was taking. I was about to leave for Australia with my boys to celebrate the Chinese New Year. I promised the team that when I came back, I would take action.

The day I returned to Hong Kong, I picked up the phone, only to be told that the CFO was still trying to move the cargo. I said to him, "You know Einstein's definition of insanity, right? It's to keep on doing the same thing over and over, all the while expecting a different outcome."

Then I asked a question that shocked him into awareness. "If you were to put *me* in your shoes, what would I do?"

Despite months of foggy thinking, he was instantly clear. Without a moment's hesitation he responded, "You'd get on a plane and go fix it."

"Then what were you waiting for?" I asked.

When he said that he'd go right away, I told him it was too late. Instead I got hold of my COO. "Do you have the required visa to go to Angola?" I asked. It turned out he did. "I want you on a plane first thing in the morning," I instructed. "You're not only going to fix this, I want you to systemize things and delegate the various tasks so it never happens again. Oh, and I want my money back."

While he was on the ground, not only did he fix the situation and systemize the operation, he got the money back. What the COO accomplished was an important lesson for the CFO, who had yet to learn what empowered people do in a crisis.

Each of us has to deal with the consequences of our actions. We can identify the options another person has, nudge, and encourage, but we can't compel them to act in their own best interest. When all is said and done, we can do everything within our range of possibilities to foster a person's empowerment, priming the pump on every level. Then, with no guarantees, we must step aside and trust.

Every child born into the world should grow up to become a person who is empowered. For the vast majority on the planet, it doesn't happen this way. The reality is that most of us who have the power to change things don't take the kind of initiative that's needed to change the current horrific state of most people's lives. The entire human race could enjoy a fantastic life in a world that's truly wonderful if we had the will to make it happen. It wouldn't even be that difficult to achieve—it's just that too few of us care enough to act.

While going inward to our center to discover what it means to be our authentic self is a vital step to becoming empowered, it's paradoxically the case that *I can only be me thanks to you.*

Without you, being me would be an isolated, unproductive experience. We can only each be ourselves because we coexist. We get to fulfill ourselves through our shared reality. In other words, as we become increasingly independent, our independence needs to contribute to the *interdependence* of our world. In more ways that we realize, truly independent people help draw out each other's interests, creativity, and skills.

Empowerment isn't an individualistic thing. It involves learning about ourselves and developing ourselves in the context of others.

12

Seeing What Others Fail to See

It's said that "luck is when preparation meets opportunity." But what exactly does preparation mean?

My answer is that preparation involves *awareness* teamed with a willingness to *embrace* whatever life may be presenting us with. Opportunities are available to everyone. The issue is whether we act on those opportunities that, once we are awake enough to spot them, are right in front of us.

This is why a tycoon I was speaking with who runs seriously large businesses remarked, "You don't need to see the road. You go forward anyway because you intuit what needs to happen, then create the road. For me, I need to see the road."

I don't need to see the road for the simple reason that I'm not fixated on where a road has to head, as long as it has the ability to bring value to people. I believe the road will be created as long as my intention is good, clear, and will benefit people. I simply create the road step by step by spotting the openings and seizing the opportunities as they unfold. This is the way of flow.

It's because of my openness to possibilities for serving humanity that much of my business has involved countries in war-torn Africa and emerging Eastern Europe. Wherever I see possibility, I create the way forward.

This is what empowered people do. They aren't dependent, sitting around waiting for God to "reveal" their path to them. They create the path based on having the courage to express what head and heart unite to show them. As the mystic Thomas Merton explains, "Looking for God is like seeking a path in a field of snow; if there is no path and you are looking for one, walk across the field and there is your path."

The truth is that I can't see anything more than you see. However, when I identify a possibility that aligns with who I am, I take the bold step of *embracing* it from a mindset of trust. Once I take this step, the clarity required to actually pursue what I'm envisioning begins to emerge. I get clear and flow into the action phase. The ability to make it happen emanates from head and heart as they unite to empower me to create what I'm seeing.

Because my aim is for everyone to live life to the fullest, which is the desire from which all of my creativity springs, I know the road will be built. This is the trust aspect. It doesn't matter that the road is probably going to start out as mud. In time we'll bring in some rocks and gravel, even though the ride will be bumpy for a while. Eventually we'll interest investors in adding a more permanent surface, and it will evolve from a one-lane road to a two-lane highway.

Even before my awakening to my authentic self, my true nature came through in aspects of my activities. One of these was that I always tried to add value to people's lives, which meant that my company never sold products that were sub-par. As you saw in the case of the notebooks, when I upped the quality, my products were always equal to or better than anything available in the marketplace at the time. Because I fully embraced what I was doing, I was committed to the highest quality, which in turn meant that I approached every-thing trustingly, instead of with the trepidation that comes from feeling threatened.

People talk about growth, having the right mindset, and preparedness for opportunity. The problem is that if you lis-ten carefully, you'll see that they have the future in mind.

When we are trusting, we do whatever is possible in *this* moment, and we don't second-guess it. We allow it to flow. Down the line, the circumstances might evolve, requiring a different decision. But we don't allow that possibility to co-opt our trust. If we don't trust, we will be unable to tap into our full resources, let alone envision the many possibilities a situation may hold. In a nutshell, to perform at our best involves showing up *in the moment,* which is what flow is all about.

The sad fact is that most are too distracted by their racing thoughts and churning emotions to spot what's staring them in the face. To allude once more to Thomas Merton's insight, they are looking for a particular mental *idea* of the path they are supposed to take instead of seeing the vast field of snow in which they can create a path. It's all about approaching situations with head and heart engaged.

When we are coming from head and heart, we look at things differently from how people generally see them. This is why I'm often able to spot opportunities in extremely uncomfortable situations, turning them to everyone's advantage.

This may sound a little weird if you haven't experienced it, but I find that as I seek to bring solutions to a given situation, in a strange way I somehow already "know without knowing" what sort of opportunity is emerging. I believe all of us possess this capacity, and it's simply a matter of tapping into our authentic essence.

A key aspect of being able to exercise trust is to be willing to know what we know. We may not have brought it into full consciousness, but deep inside we know.

I think of the story of the ancient Greek philosopher Archimedes sitting in his bathtub watching the water rise, then suddenly leaping out and running naked through the streets of Athens yelling to everyone, "I've got it! I've got it!" The rising water in the bathtub brought to full consciousness a principle he had already intuited. Isn't this how quite a lot of life works? We often know things before we *consciously* know them. This is how we can see what others don't.

How many times have you known there's a word for something you want to say, but you couldn't bring the word to mind? It happens to us all the time. We know that we know something, and yet we don't know it consciously.

This deeper knowing is the seed plot of trust. We sense something long before we realize it and move ahead based on it. For instance, don't we really know when something has ended and it's time to move on? I believe we do, at least if we are at all being real with ourselves. In the case of my marriage, I knew in my gut years before our separation that my wife and I had shifted to a different place in our lives—a place that would eventually result in going our separate ways.

It's because of the profound trust life has enabled me to develop, which has proven itself over and over in my business affairs especially, that I don't regard walking away from a situation when prudent as giving up. I see it as opening my eyes to fresh opportunities.

13

Live Your Life Free of Boxes

The way families and society as a whole tend to function, we grow up learning to live by rules prescribed by someone else instead of being guided by our own center.

Many of us begin giving away our power at a young age as we first connect with a religious institution and as a result cease being authentic. School ought to be a place where we become empowered, whereas for most of us it's where we give away still more of our power. When we go to a traditional doctor, the doctor is considered a godlike figure, so that once again we give away our power. In these and similar ways, the entire social system ends up disempowering us.

If our young people were having conversations with their instructors and classmates about the importance of tapping into the wisdom inherent in their own head and heart, ours would be a fundamentally different world. We impart a lot of information, some of which is a necessary aspect of raising educated citizens, but in most cases we fail to teach our young people how to approach life from an authentic state of being.

They learn how to earn a living, but not how to live.

I was bored during most of my years in school. The problem was that for me life has no boxes, whereas the school system teaches people to live in boxes. In this chapter, I'd like to use my own story to show how, if we are open to learn, life has all sorts of ways to set us up so that we begin to think differently and step outside our boxes.

How are we to regain our power? It involves coming to understand our fundamental godlike goodness. We each have it within us to live an empowered life in which we set our own course, increasingly living in a manner that's true to *us* instead of to someone else.

I encourage everyone who is part of a religion to ask the kind of questions I began asking back in my university days, questions that reflected my real concerns and authentic feelings such as:

- Who are you to tell me what to do? What gives you the right to order me to live my life the way you think I should live it?
- Where does the Quran say what you just said? Does it really say that, or is it just your interpretation?
- If I have the capability to make my own decisions, why do I need to ask you?

I didn't begin to have any inkling of the futility of religious rules as a guide for my life until after my university years, and even then it was only the more extreme forms that I rejected. When I was in university, I found myself moving in and out of the religious terrain, at times oscillating from one extreme to the other.

Rules don't produce good people. Have you ever noticed how those who condemn certain activities are often guilty of those same activities or similar? You see it with preachers (especially televangelists), politicians, and other breeds of moralists who seem to exist to inflict on others standards they themselves fail to maintain and sometimes glaringly flout.

When we decided to relocate to Dubai, we met a cleric who said, "If you think you are going to be able to embrace a more pure expression of your religion by moving to a Muslim country, you are mistaken. In fact, you may well move away from the faith because you are going to see Muslims doing things you would never imagine of them. Right now you differentiate yourselves, remaining firm in your beliefs, because your lives contrast with everyone around you. But when you become a part of the masses, how will you differentiate yourselves?"

The cleric proved right. Bringing our boys up in Hong Kong, we had made rules that basically said, "We don't do that because we are Muslim." All kinds of standards differentiated us as Muslims, regulating everything from what we ate to how we dressed. In Dubai we were surrounded by Muslims, some of whom didn't follow many of the rules we had been following, which meant we had to switch to telling the boys, "These are house rules, not because we are Muslims." We had gone to Dubai looking for solace in religion, but it didn't turn out to be the fulfilling experience my wife especially had hoped for.

My marriage had been drowning in rules. Life became so detail-oriented, so rule-bound, and so unforgiving that as a family we found ourselves gradually evolving away from rules for the simple reason that life was little by little showing me how nonsensical they can be. As Dr. Shefali Tsabary explains in her Oprah-acclaimed *The Awakened Family*, rules aren't a good way to raise kids because they aren't the smart way to conduct life and don't prepare our youngsters to lead successful adult lives.

I eventually came to see that all the rules, all the ways people say you have to do things, are just made up. We create our path and can devise any route we want, as long as we are authentic and have integrity. There's no rule for how things have to be. Just because somebody had a certain experience in a particular situation doesn't mean we need to also. No one can tell us how to live, no one tell us how to be. And if they try, who are they to do so? Through being loving, caring, honest, and true to ourselves, there's always a way to draw out the most human solution to each situation.

I joke with my mother and other family members, "If you do this, you get this many sawab," which essentially means credit for every good deed you do. For instance, if you went to the mosque on a particular day and prayed all night, perhaps you received the equivalent sawab of a whole year of prayer. The idea is that you have debit and credit. On your right side an angel writes down your good deeds, whereas on your left another records your bad deeds. What kind of God would operate like this?

I think you begin to see why in due course I had a major issue with religion. So when a monk inquired about my faith, I told him, "I'm a default Muslim."

I was in Bhutan, where I met many monks including the youngest reincarnate and the monk who created the Happiness Index. My sons were with me at the time and were taken aback by my statement. My sons call my mother Dadi. My younger son looked at me in shock and said simply, "If Dadi heard you, you're dead."

"I realize that," I said, "but it's nevertheless true." How could I give anything but an authentic response?

When I speak of faith, I'm not normally referring to the religious form of faith, which tends to be more a matter of believing in dogma and rules rather than practicing trust as a way of life. But does this mean there's no connection between trust and spirituality? Are the two completely different?

My former wife and I wanted our boys to be exposed to a broader view of spirituality than either of us had been brought up in. We wanted them to know about the variety of paths people follow as they seek to connect with the divine. It was important to us that they understand how various faiths think of God differently, and yet there's a common core of values—which is one of the important lessons the book and movie *Life of Pi* seek to get across. As Pi explored a variety of faiths, so also our time in Bhutan was part of a global tour of the world's major faiths. This involved visiting all the key religious sites. Iran, Syria, and Saudi Arabia were included as historical centers of Islam. We next took the boys to India to introduce them to the Hindu faith. Following this we traveled to Cusco, Peru, where we visited the different kinds of churches. We also included Laos and Cambodia, as well as Bhutan, to experience the Buddhist way.

When we depend on religion for answers, it actually handicaps us. By allowing our religion to tell us how to conduct our life, we place it in the role of making our decisions *for* us, which isn't authentic because we aren't being true to ourselves. Having someone else decide perpetuates dependence instead of fostering the ability to trust ourselves so that we are equipped to pilot our own life.

In its purest form, religion points us not to *itself* as the answer but to finding the answers within *ourselves*. It's meant to show us how to go about looking, to give us the clues so we can live a life in which we are increasingly *real*. When we instead look to a religion to regulate our behavior, it's no longer empowering but debilitating. By allowing it to hold sway in our lives, we give away our power. We are someone's puppet instead of our authentic self.

Although I told the monk who asked me about my faith that I was a default Muslim, spirituality had become far more important to me than it had ever been when I was a ritualistic Muslim. So it was that, following our world tour, we shared with the boys, "There's a sense in which you are divine, in that God is within you. You are an expression of God, kind of like a sunbeam is an expression of the sun."

After my former wife and I had introduced the boys to the

various highways to God, I explained to them, "The point is that you get to choose which path works best for you, or even whether any of these paths really work for you." To have a faith that's authentic is to be empowered to trust not only in the goodness of life but in your own essential goodness.

How many of us who attend mosques, churches, temples, and other centers of worship really experience what it is not just to try to do good, but to lead lives that are truly empowered by the goodness that's the nature of our authentic being? Because when we do, we can't help but become a powerhouse for transformation in the world. It isn't just a few good deeds we perform, it's our entire life that flows in service of our fellow humans and the planet.

Our talents, strengths, background, and opportunities need to be seen as a sacred trust. Each of us is the custodian of the wealth, the intelligence, the abilities, and everything else we possess. The point is to harness it for good, which is precisely what trust enables us to do. We are each servants of good, intended to better the lives of the whole of humanity, caring for the entire human population in all of its infinite diversity.

Although no one taught me what I'm sharing with you, it helped to have guides. I suspect we can all benefit from good teachers who have trodden the path ahead of us. But we must beware that they don't begin to take over our life and end up disempowering us. All true learning is self-directed and must allow us to make our mistakes, pick ourselves up and dust ourselves off, and move further along the path somewhat wiser. At the end of the day, only what we learn for ourselves changes us in an enduring way.

When we are guided by our own essence and its connection to the divine, we find good everywhere. We can belong to any of the many different paths and learn from all of the masters and teachers, taking with us what we find beneficial and leaving aside the rest.

How we enter into a state of trust is different for everybody. For some there's a specific moment to which they can point when the light went on for them. They suddenly woke up to see their whole life in a different light, as the teacher Eckhart Tolle describes of his own awakening in *The Power of Now*. This wasn't the case for me, as I suspect it isn't for most of us. With me it happened gradually. I became aware in one area of life, then another, followed by yet another, with the three crises I've outlined playing the key roles in this process.

One by one, each aspect of my life was being tweaked. As I embraced each shift, change happened at an accelerated rate. In due course this different way of seeing things and approaching things spread to every facet of my life. It was a process of learning how trust in life's goodness functions in each of the arenas of our everyday reality, from relationships to business, health, and our wellbeing.

All of us have a desire to be ourselves. When this is shackled, our desire finds rogue ways to express itself. The result is the selfishness and narcissism that defines so much of our world. Only when self-love is allowed free rein, so that we follow our desires in a way that requires no warping because we aren't being restricted, do we become the loving people the various religious paths urge us to be.

The most natural thing in the world is to express self-love, becoming the good person we were born to be. The most unnatural is to suppress this innate goodness by restricting ourselves to boxes.

14

Shed Your Image and Become Real

Everyone wants to improve their self-esteem, polish their self-image. The focus is on looking *at* yourself, seeing how you "come across." This is entirely different from being authentic.

I attribute a large part of my success in business to just being *real,* which affected everything I did.

Though I hadn't learned to be truly present when I was at home with my family, when I was on the ground in my work, I was *really* on the ground. I met the consumers, visiting their homes to understand their lifestyle—how they washed themselves, washed their clothes, stored their food, prepared their meals, and entertained themselves. I visited schools and got to know street kids. I had a *feel* for people's needs and the knowledge required to serve these needs. My head and heart were working in tandem. It was my grassroots understanding of what these people were about that gave me the edge.

Since I built the company, I saw it as my responsibility to know what was going on at ground level and consequently took a personal interest in how those who worked for me went about their duties. I wanted to ensure that the caring I gave to the business was happening all the way down the line to the customer on the receiving end. Ensconced in their ivory towers, many CEOs and other top-level executives in corporates are completely out of touch with this key dimension of their business. The same is true of politicians.

To make sure I was truly clued in, I majored in the element of surprise. I made sure my team never knew where I was going to show up. With a car and a driver, and speaking the local language, I could go anywhere I chose. So if there were ten routes operating on a particular day, I selected where I wanted to make an appearance. No one knew which store I might show up in at any given moment.

Despite the fact our business was significant, nobody in the countries where we operated even knew what I looked like, only that I was their biggest nightmare. You see, I never sat in the office wearing a coat and tie. Instead I used to walk the markets. Since I roamed all around the nation in jeans and a polo, no one had a clue who I was. Other than in the case of Steve Jobs of Apple, no one could imagine the big boss dressing this way, let alone trudging through the streets and sitting in open markets.

When I entered a competitor's store, the last thing they were expecting was for me to be the owner of the competition. After all, what kind of company head would show up in jeans and a polo while leading one of the top four enterprises in the nation?

Although I spoke the mother tongue of the shopkeepers, I actually didn't have to say a word to evaluate the state of play. I watched body language, not lips. How did a shopkeeper greet my team? How did everyone else in the store greet my team? What was the atmosphere like?

I was in search of a new player in one of our African markets and received the response, "Who does this guy think he is?"

I watched the shock on the faces of those present as I retorted, "Who am I? I've been supplying this market for years"

"With which product?"

"Do you happen to have seen cartons with BC markings?"

"Of course. We've sold tons of those cartons."

"Well, that's me," I said with a grin. "Bestco Continental."

They were like, "Holy shit."

Because I was intent on being genuine, image was unimportant to me. Many corporates are mostly about image, which is a feature of ego, not authenticity.

My way of developing my companies was to hire people who were good at heart—people with integrity. If you hire a good human being, you can teach them the particular skill set they require for the task. I tell people, "In business, you can't teach someone how to be a good human being—that's the job of their mother and father. But you can hire a good person and teach them a skill set." Since I started my business when I was 23, I hired people who were my age or younger—people with the flexibility, capability, and interest in progressing from being my assistant to the head buyer, or from being my merchandizer to the general manager.

Post cancer, I made the mistake of deviating from this approach. As part of my effort to find a balance between work and other aspects of my life, I began hiring highly capable people without worrying too much about their nature, especially since I hired from what were purported to be the best of the best—individuals from hypermarkets, those at the top of their game in Angola, people from the big multinationals. I built powerful teams, one in Hong Kong and one in Angola. With all of these capable people, I imagined I could delegate and be able to work less. To me, working too hard had been a major contributor to the imbalance that had destroyed my health.

I don't wish to imply that all of the big multinationals breed people who aren't good human beings. Yet the fact is, the people I hired ended up harming my Hong Kong company. For instance, our garment business is a two-season affair, summer and winter. It took only one season for me to realize that hiring such individuals wasn't working because the simple fact was that they really didn't *care* about the company, only about their income and status. Honest business—business conducted with *authenticity*—isn't just about making a profit that's fair, but about *caring*.

I'm not naive where people are concerned. At the end of the day everyone wants to help *themselves*. They want to know, "How does this further my interests? How will it improve my situation? Will it address what's important to me, helping me move forward?"

Where others are concerned, who really gives a shit about us? *We* give a shit about us, but others don't. All the talk you hear about how we're all "one," that we're essentially the same person—the idea that if you cut your arm, my arm bleeds—is just a story. How does what happens to us help anyone unless we use our experience to show caring where it's needed and welcomed?

I wanted each member of my team to do well for themselves. I'm all for supporting people's personal interests, helping them bring their dreams to fruition. If people don't care about themselves, don't look out for their interests, then they certainly aren't going to be of much use to anybody else.

But that's just the point. The *way* we promote our own interests is by caring for others. There's a synergy. You do well in business because I do well, and I do well because you do well, with both of us prospering because we are each doing well by serving each other.

If you think of all the scandals in the business world and the world of politics, how often do we see individuals, companies, even governments brought to their knees because ego took over? They create a bumpy ride for themselves and in many cases for everyone else, when all they need to do is exercise a little integrity and allow their essential goodness to do its thing.

As I shared earlier, our businesses grew because we were adding value to people's lives. We actually *cared*, actually loved what we were doing to improve life for a whole lot of our fellow humans. When you operate with integrity, what you do is pure, which eliminates the bumpiness.

With the influx into my company of new blood from the multinationals, this fundamental principle was being forgotten. What had begun as an operation that functioned more like a family was morphing into an organization in which everybody was for themselves instead of the company as a whole, let alone the public we were serving.

I don't tolerate all the politicking that goes on in many companies. I want people with heart working with me. How else can we provide a product that truly serves people's needs?

At the end I had to let the key players go. Obviously I did it ethically and politically correctly, but sadly it had to be done. To be able to function as a team player is crucial, and yet I find that many don't understand that to be part of a team should empower each team member to become more and more genuine, which is key to empowerment.

It's important for each member of the team to be able to make their maximum contribution and to do so in a manner that's both seamless and effortless. When I say "effortless," I'm referring to the experience of flow. We certainly have to put in the time needed to accomplish the tasks before us—it's not like we sit around watching movies all day. But the trick is to make the experience as energizing and fulfilling as possible. I hire people who are open to this approach and can embrace it.

I see our work as a calling, not a job. I want those who constitute my team to feel this way too. We each came to this planet to discover and develop our authentic self, then from this to serve in a way that's meaningful to us and consequently of value to others. The more we go inward, tapping into who we are in our essence, the more effectively we are able go outward in service to the world around us.

15

Tension in Relationships

Whenever I get into a relationship, I seem to lose myself, I hear people say. It happens not just in romantic relationships, but with children and their parents, friends, and people at the club...as well as in business.

While some bulldoze those who disagree with them or anyone they regard as competition, others of us are only too anxious to please, since we desperately seek approval. By capitulating to the will of others, it's easy to end up surrendering the essence of who we are.

How determined are you to hang onto what's truly important to you, staring down your ego in order to be true to yourself, while finding a way to get along well with your fellow humans? Notice I didn't say "stare-down the other person." Whether we can maintain an awareness of our authentic self in a combative situation is entirely *a matter between ourselves and our ego.*

Cooperation is rooted in strength of identity, not weakness. It involves not selling ourselves out. Someone may not like the tack we are taking, but when they see us stand up and be counted, refusing to buckle, they can't help but develop at least a begrudging respect for us as a person.

In business there's no shortage of people who will take you to the cleaners if you allow them to. My company had an exclusive agreement with a particular supplier from which we bought garments for shipments to Eastern Europe. One of our partners at the time had split, but we reconfirmed that the exclusive agreement was still in force with our company. I was well acquainted with the family who ran the company supplying the goods. The father and his sons were people you would have thought I could rely on to conduct their business with me with integrity. What a surprise to learn that they were shipping goods to my former partner.

Realizing that this was a changed situation that I needed to embrace, I requested a meeting in which I made it abundantly clear that I was immediately terminating our agreement. I actually thanked them for "kicking me in my nuts," since it provided me with an incentive to become stronger. Thus we began sourcing directly out of China, making far more money and becoming untouchable in the market from that time on.

No matter what arises, instead of allowing our ego's tendency to react to derail us, we need to look for how a changed situation can draw out more of our authentic self and embrace it, trusting that it can be turned to our advantage.

If you surrender your identity, shelving your interests in

favor of those of someone else, you'll not be happy. You'll grow to resent the situation and find yourself either bucking the person's control, with the resulting arguments and fights, or paying them back passive-aggressively. Equally, if you spurn deep connection and opt for isolation to protect yourself, you'll lose out on the fulfillment a relationship or business arrangement can bring. Internationally, it's how countries get into trade wars and embargoes in which everyone loses.

What's called for is the resilience to hold the needs of the one and the many in balance. We have to be able to flow with the current without drowning in it. This means learning to connect without losing who we are. It's in the tension between the oneness of our humanity and being an individual that meaning and fulfillment are found.

As children, we can't handle these two separate pulls of togetherness and individuality at the same time. We have to pass through various stages of development, in which each of these pulls asserts itself in a unique way, before we are equipped to balance them. When we first enter the world, we want to be held close, whereas by age two we're running in the opposite direction, doing everything the way we've been told not to do it and making great use of our favorite word, "No!" Then the whole drama replays itself in a new key, as at age three or four we don't want our parents to leave us at daycare in the morning. And so on into the teens, when at one moment we can't stand being apart from our boyfriend our girlfriend, while the next we appear oblivious of them as we pursue a sport, a career, or a night out with the guys or gals.

This struggle to be both an individual and part of the group is recapitulated in our adult relationships—and you see it writ large in business, and even larger in international relationships. The central task of life is to allow our authentic identity as a solid individual to emerge to its full potential, which is precisely what the tension between the one and the many—between the individual and family, employers and employees, or nations—is intended to tease out.

Tension in relationships of every kind is an invitation to become enveloped in the flow of the oceanic oneness, while simultaneously strengthening our personal swimming style. On the surface it may appear we are locked in a struggle for power, whether between two individuals, businesses, or nations. When viewed from the vantage of the evolutionary process, we realize the real struggle is taking place within ourselves, as we develop the strength to hold our own while connecting deeply with each other for the benefit of all.

Gabriel Garcia Marquez summed up what's occurring when he said of a character in his book *Love in the Time of Cholera*, "He allowed himself to be swayed by his conviction that human beings are not born once and for all on the day their mothers give birth to them, but that life obliges them over and over again to give birth to themselves." This is a lesson that both my personal and business relationships have been at pains to teach me through the years.

When we see humanity holistically, with each of us connected to one another at a deep core level, and we simultaneously recognize how this arrangement exists to draw out our strengths, we develop a deep respect for one another. We see the value of doing the right thing by each other, which is an act of trust.

This understanding of what's transpiring below our surface interactions changes how we look at our business competitors. Suspicion is replaced with trust. To illustrate what this means in practice, I went into the largest store in Angola, which has 14,000 square meters of floor space. I was representing Haier Group, the largest home appliances manufacturer in the world, headquartered in Qingdao, China. Glancing around, I immediately noticed there were no LG products. Locating the store manager, I asked the reason. "We haven't been approached by them," he explained.

I immediately made a phone call to the owner of the distributorship, in which I challenged, "You're not in the largest store in Angola. Are you for real? I'm standing here in the store and there's not a single LG product. I'll tell you what we're going to do. I'm going to furnish the store with your contact information and you are going to come personally and take care of this." When I got off the phone, I noticed yet another brand was missing and immediately took the same action. In fact several brands were absent.

Lacking both the trust and clarity of vision I had been blessed with, my people were freaking out. Why? Because the companies I was calling were our competitors. I handed the store owner a list of several brands he needed to stock, all from companies that were competitors, including giants like

Samsung.

Trust means we care for our customers, which requires us to empower them—the stores, and those who buy from these stores. For a store to do well, it needs to be competitive. To be competitive, the client needs a range of products to choose from. You want the customer to select what *they* wish to purchase, because no one likes to be "sold to." It's a mistake to make their choice for them by only carrying brands you want them to buy. Empowering people to make their own decisions is how you best serve them.

A store does well when customers have an array of options, which means my brand does well too. The better the store does, the better my company does, even though we're not the only line of products in the store. So when people ask me, "Why on earth would you want to foster competition?" my answer is that I'm doing the right thing by giving the customer the freedom to choose.

Because I understood the importance of differentiating myself in the market, I was never threatened by the idea of competitors. I think back to how my dad used to go to work at 7:15. At 10:00 a.m. he would break and have breakfast with the five big players—two of them Jewish, two Indian, and one Lebanese. They all enjoyed croissants and tea or coffee together. But once they left the table, they were at each others throats.

There was nothing *real* about this, nothing authentic. It was all ego. And yet the fact they met each morning revealed how, beneath all the bravado, both head and heart yearned to be part of the equation.

Instead of engaging in such hardball competition, I much prefer to simply differentiate myself in a manner that's in alignment with my true nature. The point is that when we are authentic and conduct ourselves with integrity, we feel good, which is good for our health. It's also good for business.

Whenever I went to see a potential client, I would tell them, "I'm going to look at what's best for you and your store, then see if I am part of the solution. If I conclude that what I do is what can best serve you, then great. But I'll only agree to team up with you if I'm confident this is the best way forward for both of us."

This approach, which combines both head and heart, meant that I was *already* part of the solution. It's not that you walk in and everything is instantly crystal clear. You create the opportunity to be part of the solution, then you invest the time and energy required to identify the right questions, while simultaneously becoming sufficiently aware for solutions to reveal themselves.

Given that many people, including individuals who are close to us and even family members, will try to fool us as we journey through life, using us solely for their own ends, we need to be savvy and use our head. It's a matter of being *aware* and always waiting for direction from our core self to reveal itself before we act.

In Antoine de Saint-Exupery's delightful world classic *The Little Prince*, the little fellow who has descended from the stars is in a conversation with a pilot who has crash-landed in the Sahara. On his own planet he has a rose. Since he plans to take a sheep back with him, he wants to know whether sheep eat flowers that have thorns. The pilot explains that a sheep eats whatever it finds. With his characteristic curiosity, the little prince then asks what good thorns are if a sheep can eat his rose. The pilot, upset about the bolt he can't get undone on his plane, answers with the first thing that comes into his head, telling the prince that the thorns are of no use at all. In fact, "Flowers have thorns just for spite!"

The little prince offers his own theory of why flowers have thorns—it's because they see them as formidable weapons. The symbolism is illustrative of what the situations we pass through seek to draw out in us. On the one hand they come to draw out our loveliness as represented by the rose's flowers, while on the other they can teach us to calmly stand up for ourselves and not allow ourselves to be swallowed up by another, as represented by the rose's thorns.

If you are in a situation in which someone bullies you, whether at work or at home, it's essential to be clear that this isn't acceptable. In any situation in which our boundaries are crossed, we need to show our thorns—not in an emotionally reactive manner, aggressively lashing out, but in the calm non-reactive manner of a rose's thorns. In a dangerous altercation, to show our thorns may mean to stand up for our dignity by having the courage to leave, which is exactly what my company did when we realized we were being double-crossed. It's a matter of trusting our judgment and believing in ourselves.

It's all too easy to become accustomed to being mistreated. We become so used to it that it can even begin to feel normal. If we have a tendency to act powerless, playing the victim, we need to find our center of gravity and show up with our thorns. How different this is from seeing ourselves as "abused," and labeling the one who bullies us an "abuser." These are convenient ways of sidestepping the real issue, which is our failure to take responsibility for ourselves. We prefer to act as if allowing ourselves to be abused is an addiction over which we have no control.

Relationships thrive when people are quietly strong, with their thorns in fine fettle for when they are needed. The whimperingly weak allow themselves to be walked all over. If we capitulate to an aggressor, selling ourselves out to keep the peace, we destroy the essence of what it is to relate. In fact, we're no longer relating but kowtowing.

My apprenticeship in the appropriate use of thorns began during the summer between my junior and senior years in university, when I engaged in research with a professor. I actually created my own major at Wharton, "Entrepreneurship in Family Businesses." I discovered that family-owned and closely held public corporations outperformed the S&P by a significant differential.

It happened that a multifamily office had done similar research. Thinking they would be able to impart more information than I had been able to obtain, I was grateful to be introduced to them through the family consultant with whom I was working. It turned out that I had covered more companies than they had in their research, so they decided to hire me as a consultant.

Twice a week I worked directly with the vice-president of this company. Harvard MBAs, Wharton MBAs, MIT guys, and other smart individuals were crunching the numbers. A $100,000,000 fund was launched. I got to go to New York and was involved in calls with individuals of the stature of Warren Buffet. Naturally the launch was a huge deal, with extensive press coverage the likes of The Wall Street Journal, The New York Times, and Family Business Magazine. I was surprised to find that, despite my significant contribution, there was no mention of me in any of the coverage.

When I called the vice-president, it was obvious he didn't know what to say. I suggested, "Am I to take this as an indication that I don't have a job when I graduate?" He had talked about giving me a role as assistant vice-president with a salary of $250,000. This close to graduation was hardly a good moment to wake up to the fact I had been taken for a ride.

If we're going to succeed in business or in relationships, we have to learn *not* to get taken for a ride. But this is only the first half of the equation. If not getting taken for a ride is our principal mindset, we can quickly stagnate because what's primarily driving us is fear, not trust. Success comes from transmuting fear into faith, which enables us to take a trusting approach to our journey through the world. As we allow setbacks to draw out our resilience, we move forward with increased confidence in our ability to surmount every kind of obstacle.

When you graduate from Wharton, major corporates seek you out. I had been running businesses since I was a kid, which meant I could converse skillfully during the interviews, talking about business and life in general as a pro instead of a novice in search of a job. Those I met with were well aware that I was connecting with them on their own level, which I took to be an indication that being hired was going to be a matter of where I chose to work.

When rejection after rejection began arriving, I was stunned. Picking up the phone, I made some calls to find out what in the world was going on. One of the managing directors with whom I'd smoked cigars during the interview confided, "It's simple. You're capable of telling us off if we don't make sense. We need the kind of people who listen and obey, not someone who may well disrupt the grooming process and make us look like amateurs." I adjusted my sites, opting to work with boutique firms that were happy to employ individuals who challenged the status quo.

Whereas I initially saw being taken for a ride as a setback, the discovery that I could turn even serious setbacks into springboards proved to be a major asset that was particularly valuable following the Asian financial crisis that kicked off in 1997. Working with partners who were on the ground, we started our African operations in early 2000. It was a simple matter of bringing in global brands the Africans lacked, while at the same time providing information systems, accounting systems, and control systems. It was an incredible opportunity to bring to the Third World what the First World took for granted.

By uniting head and heart, we were not only being true to ourselves but also connecting with the needs of those we served. Every seeming setback in my life has ultimately made me stronger as an individual, while helping me to serve humanity collectively more effectively.

16

Learn to Trust in the

Goodness of Life

I was speaking with a yogi, someone I have great respect for in many ways. He was a young man with a wonderful personality, who women found handsome. Nevertheless, the entire thrust of his "spirituality" ran contrary to everything I observed about him. It was all about restricting himself, limiting himself, shutting down his desires. He thought of this approach to life as "surrendering to God."

To me it indicated that he *lacked trust in the goodness of life*.

I suggest that true spirituality is all about authenticity, not at all about restricting ourselves. You only have to look at the way the world teems with innumerable expressions of creativity to see that God, or whatever term you wish to use for the intelligence in which the universe is grounded, isn't restrictive.

To live in a manner that embraces life as it unfolds will expand you, not limit you, because you will be inspired to trust. It will make your life so much easier, so much more fulfilling.

This realization of the importance of embracing each and every situation we find ourselves in led me to an axiom, and it's an important one. It's the opposite of what most believe. It's that *spirituality isn't about surrender and giving things up, but is all about opening ourselves up to receive.*

As we saw in an earlier chapter, if embracing a situation means that moving on is required, it's only to clear the way for even more worthwhile experiences to enter our life. This is something I've observed again and again in my business ventures.

A case in point is when I was asked to attend an emergency board meeting of one of our companies, where I was told that the board members were upset with my brother over an issue. Part of seeing what's really happening in a situation is to truly listen. Some of us can get to the heart of a matter and come up with a solution in no time, which spurs us to want to interrupt. I have had to stop myself, really stop myself, because for me solutions to issues tend to come quickly. I have trained myself to listen, as we all can if we once see how important it is.

The ability to really listen to one another is an art few seem to master. Equally, it's important to speak only when we have something to say that's worth others listening to. Meaningful dialogue is a matter of learning to speak to be understood and listening to understand. Our words then become significant, whereas a lot of people speak for the sake of speaking. It's so easy to fall prey to verbal diarrhea instead of giving another human being the opportunity to be heard.

When you are operating from your authentic self and not ego, you don't react to people, so I listened without saying anything. I had trained myself to get hit as hard as someone can hit me and not flinch. There were three brothers, and they were attacking my brother. "Angola and the DRC are the most profitable countries, and you and he control them," they complained. "We want to establish a policy that reinvesting retained earnings is to be determined at a board level."

When they had fully vented their grievances, I simply said, "Each of the three of you also has an older brother. Are these older brothers apprised of what you are demanding and in full agreement?" They insisted that the other brothers were all in agreement. So I said, "If I pick up the phone and ask them, they will attest to what you're saying?" They assured me this was the case.

To ask the right questions at such a moment is powerful. I therefore said, "What if I don't agree to your plan?" Not having expected me to take such a position given that they were all aligned, they were flabbergasted. They had assumed that because it was three against one, and this was backed by the other brothers, what they wanted was in the bag. "This is a board and I'm a shareholder," I reminded them, "so I have a right to agree or disagree." Since I controlled all of the supply side, I thought to myself, *If I pulled the plug and walked away, what would they be left with?*

Hearing my response, they were in shock, so I said, "Let me think about it." I didn't want to blow everything apart then and there. It was more important they learn something from this scenario, and it just so happened that the following day offered a perfect opportunity to demonstrate for them how to really play ball in the field of business we were engaged in.

Since I ran the distribution, I was the key negotiator in a deal with a potential buyer. The board watched with amazement as I negotiated for two days. The thing to keep in mind is that what had transpired the previous day didn't need to affect the negotiation. When we are real and not posturing, we treat distinct occurrences as the separate issues they actually are, instead of allowing them to become a mishmash.

If you decide to play poker, you need to be prepared for things not to go your way. You have to be ready to walk away. The simple freedom of being able to exit a situation renders you fearless, which means you don't have to try to control the outcome but can act in an empowered manner in line with what's true for you. This is trust in action.

The three brothers just assumed how I would act, never thinking through the "what ifs" of the situation. These same partners had objected when I reduced the number of items we were selling in Africa because I preferred to focus on quality cargo that would improve people's lives. Based on the concept that less is more, I had reduced the 1,500 items they had been carrying to 150. Year on year we made more and more money, while we better served the needs of more people, thereby transforming lives.

Our mission was to provide quality products at affordable prices to improve the quality of life. I should point out that the 150 products we were bringing in were new to the market, not simply part of the 1,500 they had been selling. We were developing new categories in the market. The brothers had been extremely upset at the time I made these changes because they wanted me to import products that everybody and their grandmother could import under a different brand name. I wanted to give the African people a different experience, not just cheap copycats.

Whether in our families or going into a business meeting, our part is to give 100 percent in each and every moment. When we are fully engaged in this way, truly listening and aware, we will experience no panic if the time comes either to walk away or to let go of something we have invested in. We know it's going to be okay.

To trust is perhaps the most important lesson we can ever soak up from the experiences life sends us. To know that with relationships, business, or any other aspect of life, there's a time to simply walk away and move on in trust is one of the most vital insights to impart to our young people. It would spare them so much despair, giving them hope and a sense that their lives have meaning. Without trust we are at risk of going into a downward spiral.

Trust leads to clarity, which leads to action. A week after the altercation with the three brothers, I flew to Paris and bought out one set of partners. The next day I flew to Canada and bought out the other set of partners. Having listened closely to what was actually being said, the various incidents had shown me that it was time to move on.

The relevance of this is the importance of learning to sit and listen without reacting, even when you are being hammered on an issue. If someone is upset, I say nothing and simply let them get it all out. Afterwards we look at the issue and reflect on what needs to happen in order to move forward.

I want to be clear that I'm not talking about numbing yourself during an attack. On the contrary, I'm talking about being alive, fully attuned to what's transpiring, with both head and heart engaged. I allow myself to feel everything with its full force. Reacting isn't at all helpful and may ignite a war. But when we can feel the pain at such times and not tune it out, we open ourselves to identify a way forward.

We also enhance our ability to feel the joy of life because we are learning to experience *everything* more fully.

I could never have imagined the path that was about to open up as I began stepping through the snowfield of that board meeting. Because I embraced each step as it unfolded instead of fighting the situation, it led to an opportunity for expansion—and the opportunity for increased service of my fellow humans—beyond my wildest dreams.

17

Flow Is a State of
Relaxed Intensity

Straddling life and death as I did when cancer struck can take you into such a state of shock that you have to relearn the basics. It's akin to shattering your leg in an accident and having to relearn how to walk, or suffering a stroke and being forced to learn how to talk all over again.

The trick post-cancer was to find a balance. I needed to relearn authentic decision-making, while at the same time I needed to back off from my former level of intensity. As I experimented, I gradually relaxed into my work. The *feeling* aspect of my authentic self was progressively deepening, which meant I recognized the importance of caring for myself.

For two years after remission I wasn't allowed to travel to Africa. Within six months of remission, we had exited every country except Angola and Namibia. In due course I began to visit Angola five times a year. I would go for two weeks at first, then I cut down to twelve days, ten days, nine days, and finally eight days only three times a year. I was becoming more proficient in operating from the state of flow. As a result, the business expanded year on year, improving on every level and becoming easier to manage. It was sort of scary to watch it. I was like, "How is this happening?"

Instead of being driven as I once was, I was no longer fixated on "getting somewhere." Unlike so many who hope to someday "arrive," I was increasingly able to relax while being fully present, which allowed me to embrace the journey more than ever. Soon this began to spill over into other aspects of my life.

There needs to be a consistency to all we do. At work, at home, and in our social life, the same authentic and relaxed person needs to show up. This means becoming *real* in everything.

When we are true to ourselves, we are still part of our family, still a member of our community, still involved in the business world, but there's no image to portray, no posturing required, which removes all the drivenness from whatever we engage in. Living in the state of flow, we don't get caught up in the hardness of life but remain in the soft, open space. We are an ambassador for the quiet way, the peaceful way, the calm way, the way of gentleness instead of the harshness of so much of society. It's the opposite of the anxious—I would even say *tormented*—state so many exist in.

Until cancer struck, I lived a compartmentalized life in which my work life and home life were separate. To see what this looks like, imagine yourself on a dinner date when your spouse asks you a question. You are so immersed in thoughts about your business that you answer with, "Huh?" When my wife repeated her question, I gave the same response, "Huh?" Having been ignored twice, she simply gave up, and I can't blame her.

Being at work and being at home are two different aspects of life, but they shouldn't be two different versions of who we *are*. Both should reflect our integrity, each a relaxed expression of ourselves.

We require a certain passion for impactful work, but we also need an equal amount for home life. We need a relaxed intensity in both aspects of our life, so that we approach each with a certain spiritedness. It's about taking a holistic approach to our lives.

True, our energy in the evening may not be of the identical calibre of the morning, when we are keyed up. It's appropriate for the evenings to be more relaxed, which is why our cortisol level drops gradually from when it surges in the mornings to awaken us. Nevertheless, mentally, emotionally, and spiritually, I'm clear that when I enter the door following my workday, it's not couch potato time but game time.

To promote an appropriate relaxed intensity for each aspect of my life, I took up meditation. After I had been meditating every morning and every evening for a couple of years, which served to balance the sympathetic and parasympathetic aspects of my autonomic nervous system—my use of my accelerator and brake—I underwent training in Los Angeles with a leading memory and speed-reading expert, Jim Kwik.

Utilizing an instrument called the Muse, he measured my mental stability in terms of my degree of calmness. I was interested to see what the sensors on my scalp would pick up, since this was the first time I had received feedback regarding my brain activity.

I was now two years into my separation, and this was ten years after my diagnosis with cancer. The equipment graded anxiety levels as active, neutral, and calm. I measured 50 percent calm, 47 percent neutral, and three percent active. The active reading was the result of hearing what I deemed to be a scream, or at least a drastic raising of a voice, twice during the process. On both occasions the activity in my brain went haywire, whereas otherwise it was either neutral or calm.

A few months later, I underwent a brain scan with Dr. Daniel Amen. "Your brain looks beautiful," I was told. The technicians had measured my anxiety. When you have a significant amount of anxiety, it shows up on the scan as a diamond. I have a picture of my scan and you can see the diamond clearly. I inquired, "Is this from the cancer or from the divorce?" Unfortunately it wasn't possible to put a timeline on it. It revealed only the present state of my brain.

After I had become ill a decade earlier, as part of my recovery I read many books and engaged in various types of training, along with engaging personal coaches to address different aspects of my life. I wanted to understand what had led to having ten tumors at the young age of 35.

We know that our DNA can exhibit certain tendencies, but this isn't a death sentence. Not just nature is at play in illnesses such as cancer, but also nurture. This is why people with identical predispositions can experience entirely different outcomes. The real issue is what part nurture plays in triggering or accelerating a particular process.

When I speak of nurture, I'm including such matters as diet, sleep patterns, whether we work out, our mental and emotional state, along with whether we enjoy meaningful connections with others. While these can be difficult to quantify, technology is aiding in this. For instance, in no other era was it possible to monitor a person's sleep patterns in a lab, yielding a wealth of information. As just one example of a valuable finding, it's now known that many suffer from sleep apnea, which is a contributor to hypertension, leading to heart attacks, stroke, liver problems, and other potentially deadly conditions. This is insight people need.

When you consider all the money poured into education—the years invested in going to school to develop the intellect, work skills, and to a limited degree social skills—it makes no sense that we spend almost no time focusing on mental and emotional hygiene. We don't teach our children how to be passionate but also relaxed. Yet these are the aspects of our makeup that are the most impactful where health and wellbeing are concerned.

We now know that how we feel—whether we are stressed, anxious, angry, or depressed—has a huge effect on our wellbeing. If you stop to consider, it's obvious this is the case, even before science demonstrated the veracity of this finding. How could the way we feel not affect our wellbeing when it's something that's with us every moment?

Currently most people have no system in place to help process their feelings, other than seeking out some form of counseling once their mental state has already deteriorated. We go from week to week, month to month, even year to year experiencing emotions that are detrimental to our well-being, but we fail to bring these onto the front burner so that they can be addressed. Why wouldn't we treat such matters as urgent, when not only the quality of our life but also our longevity is affected?

We show up at work with particular skill sets, a background in a relevant field, and a certain level of experience. But what about the feelings we bring to our place of work, and those emotions that arise throughout the day, each and every day? If we are to add value to society through our work, aren't these at least as important as our skills, our background, and our experience?

Chatting with an extremely driven 36-year-old who runs a bank, he confided that about every third day he doesn't go home for dinner but goes out to eat. "I need a change of scenery," he explained.

"You have a loving wife and kids, and you have a beautiful house," I challenged, "so why the need for a change of scene every third day?"

"Yeah, yeah, it's not that," he said. "It's that my office is shit, and the market is what it is. I have a hundred things I need to do, a hundred reasons to be at my desk from 8 a.m. to 7 p.m. I even eat at my desk."

Venturing where angels fear to tread, I suggested, "You might want to look into that."

"I have to meet my numbers every year, year on year," my friend retorted. "That's what I *do* every year."

"I get it," I said. After all, what he was doing had been my life at one time. Still, it was quite something to see his absolute resistance to what I was suggesting.

I persisted, "You've been doing what you are doing for the last how many years? So, is it really serving you? Is this what you want to do for the rest of your time on earth? Is it truly the optimal approach? Do you really even want to do it at all, or is that you're stuck and merely going through the motions? I'm just asking you to reflect."

"I don't want to be a pinball between home and work," he lamented, "which is what I feel like. I need a third place to go."

"You tell me that you're doing all this stuff for your wife and kids," I challenged, "and yet you bring home only the stale, perhaps somewhat jaded, maybe even angry side of you. In other words, those you love most get to bathe in the toxic residue of your day. Where's the sense in that?"

I think of a daughter-in-law whose mother-in-law was in hospital in Hong Kong. Since she was alone with the mother-in-law, her husband called me one evening seeking my help. The daughter-in-law watched as I sat next to the mother, held her hand, and gently kissed her forehead. As a result of observing the dynamic in the hospital room, a couple of days later the daughter-in-law showed up in my office. The reason she had come was that she saw the connection in the hospital room. She needed help she said.

It was actually seeing me in action, seeing the connection for herself, that moved her to seek help. She began to understand what it feels like to really care for someone. We spoke for a couple of hours, then I called her the next day and spoke to her for a further hour and a half.

She happened to be a leadership coach and was working with some quite large companies. Back in that environment, it was as if everything we had tapped into in the hospital room, in my office, and on the phone never happened. The softness was gone and the hardness was back. How easily our old brain patterns reassert themselves when we first begin to recognize the need for a paradigm shift in our lives.

I have birthed several businesses, and I now know they can be created without all of the drivenness that characterized my earlier years and led to cancer and finally divorce. All we need to do is proceed step by step, relaxing into each moment, which provides us with the clarity required to leverage each opportunity as it arises from flow. The same is true for our home life.

What's required of us in *any* aspect of our life is that we are actually *present* at any given moment, ready to trust and enjoy a relaxed intensity that enables us to live in such a manner that we are fully alive.

18

Banish Mediocrity

One of the principal lessons of the experience of marrying, raising a family, and ultimately divorcing has been to arrive at the place where I'm comfortable enough with myself that I can express myself without reservation. Society's approval of my decisions has become irrelevant to me because I've been through so much that has taught me the importance of being me.

I like what Warren Buffet says, "Be yourself because everyone else is taken." Why would we want to be anybody else? I am who I am, and if someone doesn't like it, *c'est la vie*.

Each of us should have the right to be who we are, which is the exact opposite of the conformity the social order promotes. To be authentic is paramount. Of course, I'm referring to our true self, not the ego's "I gotta be me" counterfeit of authenticity, which is what leads to people being rude, hurtful, and intrusive where others are concerned.

Almost every aspect of our social and educational structures is geared to getting us to fit in, which requires us to suppress what we really feel, really want—in fact, just about everything we truly desire. We end up becoming this "other person." Then one day the life our ego has built comes tumbling down—perhaps through divorce, illness, our kids getting into trouble, or a business reversal. As we wake up to how false it has all been, we look back at ourselves and wonder, "Who the hell was that person?"

I have had to weigh many a situation to determine what authenticity required of me and what would constitute compromising myself. This has been especially true of my business dealings.

In the early 1990s, Chinese businessmen used to be pissed with me because I wouldn't smoke with them, drink with them, or womanize. I would get asked, "Why are you here? We don't do business with people like you." Of course, when I suggested I could leave, it was a different story. The fact that I refused to play their game didn't alter their need for the amount of business I brought them. This was an era when a lot of the companies were owned by the state, which meant that going out for a meal was basically an opportunity to party.

Not drinking was even more of an issue when I went deep into Eastern Europe and even further east, where unless you drank you literally weren't welcome. I was in Azerbaijan having lunch and everybody got half a bottle of vodka with the meal. They actually drank in the name of the Prophet. Each rose to give a toast, following which everyone took a shot.

My non-participation irked them. Because I was so strict in those days, I refused to pay for alcohol even when guys from the multinationals were out eating with me, requiring any alcohol to be billed separately because I didn't wish to support their drinking. It's different from my approach today, since these days I'm much less interested in controlling others.

To be in integrity, we must dialogue, negotiate, and render the best decisions we can at any given moment, always with the awareness that life isn't a fixed entity but an ongoing process, which means that what's right for this moment may not be right for tomorrow. Through love, honesty, and just being ourselves, there's always a way to draw out the most human solution in a given moment.

It seems to me that not many of us really spend time examining our lives, making an effort to know ourselves and what's important to us, as well as to be clear about what we *don't* like.

A great deal is said about the need to compromise. I prefer to negotiate, which is much different from compromise. Suppose you want beef for dinner, whereas I want potatoes. Shall we compromise and make a hash of our dinner?

Negotiation involves discerning what's truly important and therefore nonnegotiable for each party. When I negotiate, I don't allow myself to be derailed by meaningless issues. I'm going for win-win on the things that really matter, not settling for the lowest common denominator associated with all the less-essential side issues.

When I seek a win-win solution to the various situations

that require negotiating, the aim is for each of the partici-
pants to come away from the table with what's truly important to them. This requires each of us to first identify what's
essential, then secondly to let go of those things we might like
but that aren't crucial to the negotiation. To achieve this, we
brainstorm with everything on the table. We leave no stone
unturned. As we listen with real openness, invariably a path
opens up that no one imagined possible. Either that, or we
decide to take different paths.

Contrary to what it may appear on the surface, this is
much more about *ourselves* than about the other. It has to do
with how willing we are to challenge ourselves. Is a decision
we are making really the wise choice? Does it truly represent
our core or some aspect of ego to which we are still holding
on? Unless we're willing to explore our own depths, how are
we to know?

When an international hypermarket wanted to buy one of
our companies, one of my conditions was no cigarettes, alcohol, or pork to be sold. I believed that if I made money from
something against my values, the money would be tainted.
My dad wouldn't even sell playing cards when he was in business because he knew they may be used for gambling. Others
took the approach, "I don't drink, smoke, or gamble, but it's
okay to sell these items."

We used to import clothing to Eastern Europe that wasn't
only for the mamas but also for those who were fit, which
meant that some of it was pretty skimpy—certainly not items
I would want any member of my family to wear. This led to

a debate. If we could sell clothes that were unorthodox, what was the difference between this and selling cigarettes and alcohol?

Where do you draw the line when it comes to items that may be harmful? Everybody draws the line somewhere, but in many cases it's blurry. There's no rule for how things have to be. There may not be easy answers on many issues, but it's essential we engage the questions and not just slough them off and settle for a mediocre way of doing things. Mediocrity is the result of compromising ourselves. I believe we compromise largely because of fear. Not just fear of what the other person might think of us, but fear of laying claim to our greatness and therefore going after the things that really matter to us.

The fact is, fear causes many of us to resist feeling really good. If this weren't the case, our world would be in a different state because we wouldn't tolerate the mess it's currently in. We wouldn't put up with the mediocre nature of the lives the majority lead. This state of resistance that entombs so many of us means we don't aspire to live an extraordinary life. We are so unaccustomed to living in an extraordinary manner that we don't believe it possible. We have been schooled to expect and settle for the lowest common denominator.

The message from so many quarters is, "Don't expect too much from life. Be content with what you have." Well, yes, there's a role for contentment. It's needed when you are in a situation you can do nothing about. But it should never become an excuse for putting up with the awful state in which most on the planet exist. I've had to be content at times, but I never tried to make out that it was some sort of spiritual ideal. I saw these times for what they were—the travesty of humans settling for atrocious conditions, when with just a little creativity, caring, and effort things could be drastically different. Remember, where there's a will, there's a way.

Even when contentment is called for, I make the situation the *best* it can be. It's a matter of being realistic about life's various situations and coming up with the best solution possible given the circumstances. You have to try to find the humanity in a given situation, whether it's for yourself or for another.

To show you how this works in real life, in the early 1990s I was in Eastern Europe. A lot of the meat dishes were built around pork. I ate only vegetables and fish when I ate out, which in that context made for scant pickings.

If you order minestrone in most venues imagining you are eating vegetarian food, think again. I was sitting with Matthieu Ricard at TED Global when he ordered the minestrone. "Wait a minute," I interrupted, turning to address the waiter as I inquired, "What's the broth?"

"Always chicken broth," the waiter said proudly. He was taking a meal order for a monk and didn't make the connection to the fact Buddhist monks are vegetarian. This wasn't a hole in the wall, where you might expect them not to know. This was the Copacabana Palace. We had a good laugh about it during the dinner.

Scientists have conducted studies of Matthieu—brain

scans in which the equivalent of a bomb goes off, and he doesn't flinch. Based on extensive testing, he's been classified as "the happiest man in the world." We're talking about an individual who has engaged in not 10,000 hours of meditation but way over 50,000.

You have to know what matters—what would compromise who you *are*. Coinciding with the publication of his book, Matthieu was to go on the road giving talks and interviews. Following this he was scheduled to go into hibernation, far up the mountains of Tibet. His months of hibernation are something like January, February, and March if I recall correctly. I said to him, "Matthieu, are you crazy? It's freezing up there at this time of year."

His response revealed he understood what matters. "It's better if it's cold, because you can keep yourself warm, than having to deal with mosquitoes and flies in the summertime," he explained. The comical aspect of this is that here you have a human being who takes off two to three months to be on his own, speaking to no one, yet he's smart enough to do it at a time when it's going to be "easier." We all like our touch of luxury. And why not?

In the early 1990s, I flew to Shandong province in China to buy notebooks. Following our meeting, my supplier dropped me at the airport. Mobile phones were new and I didn't yet own one. Consequently I had no idea our flight had been delayed almost six hours until I had already been dropped off at the curb. In due course the airline handed each of us a lunchbox. An airport lunchbox in those days was barely edible.

I was really hungry, so I stepped out of the airport, hailed a cab, and told the guy to just drive. At the time few foreigners ventured to this region. Since I barely spoke any Chinese and the driver didn't speak any English, we drove until I spotted a restaurant. When I conveyed to him that I wanted him to come inside with me, I'm sure he thought I was nuts.

It was a true hole in the wall with no menu. Using sign language, I requested that I be allowed to go in the kitchen. Taking a bunch of vegetables like broccoli, beans, and a leafy green, I found some garlic and gestured to the kitchen staff to make me a stir-fry accompanied by rice. I should have omitted the rice because rice in China in those days resembled pebbles, not very edible. After my taxi driver and I had eaten, he took me back to the airport.

Was I just being a spoiled brat? Or was it a matter of honoring our humanity by not compromising ourselves? When it comes to food, comfort, the kind of hotel we stay at, the car we drive, or the service we receive, is luxury such a bad thing?

My answer is that it depends on whether it's a matter of respect for ourselves or simply ego. The litmus test is whether we are able, as someone said wisely long ago, to "be both abased and to abound." Can we be emotionally okay with being at either end of the spectrum according to what circumstances dictate and there's no way to change them? Is there a certain contentment in us regardless of the external situation?

I find that I can do both—be abased *and* abound. But there's no question which I have a preference for, as we all would had we not been trained to accept conditions that are contrary to our wellbeing and a betrayal of our humanity.

I need to add one other insight regarding why I don't compromise myself. The moments when life seems perfect can feel almost *too* good—so much so that it can be scary, unaccustomed as we are to feeling fantastic. No sooner do we begin to experience happiness than we invariably start asking ourselves, "Okay, what's going to happen next?"

God forbid we should ever feel sustained bliss or ecstasy, because we'd be beside ourselves with worry about when the other shoe might drop and deprive us of the fulfillment we're enjoying.

Don't you find this a strange reaction? Why wouldn't we simply bask in a state of gratitude? I think of a couple of writers who point out just what an enigma it is that we're so fearful of feeling fantastic. Emerson spoke of being "glad to the brink of *fear*." The poet Denise Levertov penned the words, "Thrust close your smile that we may know you, *terrible* joy."

Why do we think of happiness as fleeting, fulfillment as unsustainable, and ecstasy beyond tolerating for more than the few seconds in an experience such as orgasm? Only because we have lost touch with our joyous, ecstatic, blissful center—the person we *really* are, which tolerates no mediocrity and never compromises ourselves.

19

What's All the Sadness About?

Faced with loss—the loss of our job, our financial security, a valued possession such as our home, or especially a loved one whether to death or a breakup—if we experience a tremendous emptiness and the sense that our world has collapsed, as I did when my wife announced she was leaving me, what we are encountering is the hollow space within ourselves where our real self failed to develop during childhood.

The hollowness we feel at our center when we don't know our authentic self is the root of the neediness and ego that drives so much of the behavior we see in business and relationships. It's what pushes some to the point of murdering a spouse or lover who leaves them, so overwhelming is it to be fully exposed to the pain of our missing self.

When we aren't in touch with who we really are, relationships more than anything else in life provide a transfusion of selfhood. We *borrow* a sense of identity from the other, by which I mean that it's their presence in our life that gives us meaning. As long as we have someone in our life to fill the void, a career to keep us busy, and entertainment to take our mind off the emptiness within, we don't tend to notice just how much we are hurting.

In addition to the transfusion a relationship can provide, some of us shop to fill the void, others of us drink or eat in excess, while still others of us chase after sex, do drugs, expend our energy trying to control the people in our life, or in other ways stay busy. Without these things, we would feel the emptiness we so dread and will do just about anything to avoid.

A borrowed sense of self is never an enduring, deeply satisfying experience but constantly has us on a knife's edge. We're forever at risk of the transfusion of selfhood from the other's presence being withdrawn. This of course is what leads to trying to please the other by becoming compliant. We don't want to lose them, so we try to please in order to get them to stay.

This selling out of ourselves to the other is why so many feel they lose themselves whenever they get into relationships. It's also what leads to arguing and fighting, as each tries to impose on the other. The urge to control stems from the neediness I talked about a moment ago. It's this neediness that fuels our possessiveness, jealousy, impatience, pouting, anger, and other destructive emotions.

If the transfusion of selfhood is withdrawn, such as in a breakup, it inevitably feels as though the lifeblood is draining from us. The result is that we suffer terribly, as I did during those three years after my marriage broke up.

When we're bereft, distraught, believing our life to be without meaning any longer because of the loss of someone dear to us, *the loss mirrors an emptiness within us that has been there all along.* We are made acutely aware of our missing self.

At the resort where I began writing this book, during one of my morning yoga meditations involving an exercise for the throat chakra, I unexpectedly began coughing. Not just the kind of cough we all experience at moments to clear our lungs or throat of excess mucus, but a bout of real coughing. When it finally ended, I found myself feeling sad. What triggered this?

When my beloved chose not to join me at the resort, the sadness I experienced was entirely different from the bereft feeling during the years following my wife's decision to leave. I didn't feel at all hollow inside. Because I no longer needed to borrow a sense of self, I was able to appreciate the resort, since beneath the feeling of missing her was the joy of simply being *alive* and being *me.*

And yet, to be without this woman on this most important project for which I had waited more than seven years was sad. I began to understand that feeling bereft and feeling sad are fundamentally different.

Approaching everything in life from our authentic self enables us to trust the intelligence behind the universe, an intelligence in which all authenticity is grounded. We trust what *is,* allowing it to simply *be* without fighting it. We remain open, letting situations work themselves out in whatever direction they may take. When we do this, the right solution will always come. What needs to happen emerges when the time is right.

I was learning to give up on needing to know where things are going ahead of time and simply trust. The path forward would make itself known, as I had learned from a number of situations in my life in which I wasn't in a place where I could understand what was transpiring. I'm sure you've been in the kind of situations in which you can't gauge things. As we transition from control to trust, it can be quite challenging. However, once we master the art of trusting, it's actually a far easier route through life because it takes the worry out of it.

I sent a text to my beloved that simply stated, "I hope you're okay."

"Don't you worry about me, I'm great," she texted back. "I'm with friends and family."

It didn't matter whether I really believed my beloved was "great." The reality was that it didn't actually matter that she could say she was great. It wasn't my place to believe or not believe her. Given that I *wasn't* that great, all I needed to do was take care of myself. I didn't want to be great just then, only to feel what was happening in all of its rawness.

Sitting with the sadness, allowing it to simply be what it was, I realized I felt calm, peaceful, even content. When I saw the doctor again and she checked my vital signs, she told me, "You're quite still inside. Even though you're going through something so sad, you're calm."

Sad, but not fighting the sadness—just allowing it to sit

side-by-side with my interest in the project I was engaged in—I settled down to work. In this time of sadness, all that mattered was for me to be the loving and creative person I inherently am.

In due course my beloved sent a further text in which she said, "I love this time of year. I love to celebrate and be celebrated during this time of year. I just wish it was with you." It was now that I realized how *I* was completely there with her in the relationship, while also at peace with her *not* being with me. This is what allows us to be present in whatever we are doing.

The difference between missing our own self and missing another person is night and day. When we don't know our true self and someone goes out of our life, it's not so much that we miss the person for who *they* are. It isn't missing the person in their own right that causes the acute suffering we experience. The pain is coming from the removal of the stop-gap they have been providing in the absence of being present for ourselves. But when our authentic center comes into its own, and we then lose someone from our life, we actually miss *the person* for who *they* are, rather than for what they do for our personal sense of self.

Unlike our fragile ego, which reacts with strong emotion to unpleasant situations, our authentic self is capable of feeling really, really deeply. Instead of the kind of self-pity our ego indulges in, such as telling ourselves "I'm all on my own," I was experiencing genuine sadness that the two of us weren't together. We had enjoyed so many incredible moments that I was sad to be denied the opportunity of creating more such moments. Despite everything I had done in my life, all the adventures I had participated in, I had never before had an opportunity to create experiences in which we both enjoyed such a high degree of alignment.

No matter how much we enjoyed each other's presence, I recognize how mistaken it is to imagine we can "give someone our heart." This is nothing but emotional enmeshment, whereby two people become confused about who each of them really is. We are ever and always individuals—as divorce painfully proves to half of us, while many of us will discover it when one or the other of us passes.

The concept of "giving someone our heart" is a reflection of neediness on the part of two people who haven't yet discovered their own center and are seeking to borrow a sense of self from each other. It's entirely different from sharing ourselves with another from a sense of our own fullness.

This is why so many who are in relationships become resentful and pout if they don't feel they have all of the other person—if the person also has other people or activities that are important to them. Wanting someone's total attention is needy behavior, not love.

We can walk through life holding hands, but we can never possess the other's heart. On the contrary, our heart must always remain ours, for how else can love flow from us to another? The key to abiding love is to own more of our heart as our life moves forward, not less. Only in this way can we love unreservedly.

Love is an appreciation for who a person is, not for what they complete in us. Our partner's wider life is thus embraced as enriching the primary relationship, since their contact with others and involvement in projects that interest them draws out more of who they are as a person, which then feeds back into the romantic connection we relish with them.

Love, caring, and consideration aren't like a bank account whose funds can be drained. They aren't finite, in limited supply. If we find our ability to love restricted in some way, *we* are creating that restriction. The divine that's the source of love in each of us knows no such restriction.

Our authentic self is able to consider everyone's needs and willingly accepts the emotional pain of having someone withdraw their love. This is possible because the love we feel when we come from our authentic self is unilateral and not dependent on the availability or mood swings of the other.

If we truly love someone, we continue to love them even if they pull away, which means we feel the sadness that accompanies the absence of their wonderful presence in our life and all the joyous aspects of ourselves their presence draws out. There's no punitive reaction on our part, no closing off to the person, no shutting down of our feelings and lapsing into a state of numbness. As I pointed out earlier in the book, this is why I continue to show considerable care for my former wife even though it's now some years since we divorced. Genuine love never dies, although the form it takes may change.

To be nonattached is the way of our authentic self and runs counter to the ego's way of manipulating situations to corner what it wants. But let me be clear that when I use the word "nonattached," to be attached isn't at all the same as experiencing a deep connection. To be attached is to be emotionally enmeshed, whereby neither party functions from a state of emotional independence. It's leaning on each other for our sense of self. Instead of a healthy interdependence, we experience an unhealthy sense of propping each other up emotionally.

Paradoxically, to be nonattached is what allows us to become profoundly connected. Because we are free of a need for the other, we can afford to love unilaterally at those times when the other shifts into ego and consequently doesn't feel loving toward us. How we feel about the other isn't dependent on how they treat us. Our feelings for them are quite separate from how they may be feeling or how they are behaving. Thus to be nonattached is the exact opposite of apathy or shutting down. The antithesis of numbness, it's a complete aliveness in all our senses.

Thus my beloved's absence from the resort where we had planned to be together didn't cause me to shut off my feelings, but on the contrary allowed me to experience just how much I wanted to be with her—wanted her to be in my life. Wanting isn't drivenness, neediness. It's appreciating who someone is in their true being, then enjoying their presence in our life to whatever degree they are willing to share themselves.

20

An Extraordinary Life Is About
We, Not Just Me

When people awaken to the need for some form of spirituality in their life, the focus initially is usually on "me." It's perfectly natural for it to begin with "me," but eventually this needs to expand to include "we."

As we begin to uncover a new sense of ourselves based on authenticity, there can be a tendency to dismiss our past. We fail to appreciate that the past is the foundation on which the future rests, especially where the "we" is concerned. If we are to become fully developed human beings who are able to really care about and contribute to the wellbeing of others—"we" and not just "me"—it's important not to put down our less-authentic earlier days. Far from being of little value, they were an important steppingstone.

Disowning our past can too easily constitute shutting the door on our feelings, which is the antithesis of becoming real. We have only to think back to our childhood to realize that we all have significant memories of this kind of lopping off of our feelings, which in different ways and to varying degrees has been going on all our lives. Those occasions we remember tend to be paradigmatic.

In my late teens, I used to spend my weekends taking my cousins to movies, malls, amusement parks, and skiing. They were six, seven, eight years younger than me. Then came a family crisis and it all stopped. One of the mothers basically discounted everything I had done, as if all that I did wasn't done from my heart. She seemed incapable of grasping that everything I did was because I *chose* to do it. Why else would I spend my time with cousins years younger than myself instead of hanging out with my own age group?

In my teens, I was strong and from time to time used to carry my mother in my arms, kind of like you carry a child. One day when I was around 17 or 18, she said, "Stop this. You're not a kid anymore." It was hurtful to be pushed away like this.

These two incidents caused something inside me to shut down. I built a wall around myself, which meant I didn't ever truly hug my mother again for years. Later I taught our boys to really hug, holding the person for nine or ten seconds. When they initially did this with my parents, you should have seen my mother and father's heads! They were looking around like squirrels, not knowing what to do with themselves. I'm pleased to say that today they enjoy being hugged, really hugged.

I find it unbelievable that we can be the center of someone's life, then nothing. After perhaps 15 years, we simply press control-alt-delete, then pivot. How can we be so hard toward someone who for a long time made us feel incredible? I'm so willing to forgive and forget, remembering the good times spent with the other, and in that spirit to help each other move forward into a new phase of our journey. I encourage you to find it within you to be the same.

I'm often stunned by how little people seem to mean to one another, not only in families and friendships but also in the workplace. I had a general manager who worked with me for 20 years. We traded together, ate incredible food, had the most amazing adventures, laughed, played poker with suppliers, and endured periods of severe stress. But when we sold the company and she started to work for the company we sold to, I never saw her once. How could we go from trusting one another in everything to, "Okay, whatever"? Human hearts are surely bigger than this.

In business, if I really thought about whether the other person cares the same as I do, I would actually be depressed because I'm quite sure most don't. Most of them are there just for the deal. My team used to tell me, "You really care, but I don't think they do."

I could of course conclude that I live in Lala Land. Or is it that caring is what our *real* self is all about, but few of us are sufficiently in touch with this aspect of ourselves at this stage in the evolution of our species? We are still in large measure in the "me" part of our journey, not yet "we."

Coming to the place in life that "we" governs how we approach things exerts a defining impact on how we function in the business world. Running a business, everybody needs to matter—our team, our clients, the distributor, the seller, the end customer. The consumer is seen as a gift, which means we don't think about a transaction either in terms of doing people a favor or seeing what we can get from them. Real service means that I appreciate you. I'm thankful to be here for you as a servant in this moment in time.

I have a tremendous appreciation for the vast experience my years in business brought me, both in Eastern Europe and Africa. They laid the foundation for the birth of my present work, for I could not have built Qineticare without what my experiences taught me. Not only did they fund Qineticare, which meant I could develop it without compromising anything I do for financial reasons, they also enabled me to discover and hone the skills I now use each day to serve not only individuals but their multigenerational families, which are in many cases spread across the globe.

As I shared in an earlier chapter, when I launched my businesses in Africa, my aim was to make available to the Third World what the First World takes for granted. My mission was to improve the quality of the lives of the African people one product at a time, and to do so with care and compassion. For example, in Eastern Europe there were no mass market brands of clothing in the early '90s. We enabled the ordinary person to enjoy fashion in a way only the few had so far been able to experience. We also made brands like Disney and Warner Bros. accessible and affordable to children.

My experience in these emerging markets allowed me to understand both the limitations and the opportunities of these countries. I developed an acute ability to see what was possible in a region that had no exposure to such possibilities. Our company was able to imagine and then create a different quality of life for the average person.

Through entering into and developing these markets, I learned a great deal about crisis management, as you read about earlier in the book. This opened my eyes to see the vital importance of preparing ourselves and our loved ones for the challenges that life inevitably sends our way. My own financial, health, and relationship crises further honed the skill set that presently enable me to serve many families around the world through Qineticare, the world's first family health office. We are able to assist many in taking the practical steps that are essential for a more conscious approach to the physical, mental, emotional, and relational wellbeing of the individuals and their families at large.

I hear people say they are moving up in their level of consciousness. That may or may not be the case. Labeling in this way can be just another form of ego. "Higher" and "more evolved" are evaluations made by ego, not the true self, which knows and trusts that whatever comes next is what's needed. It's important to embrace and celebrate the whole of our journey not only conceptually, but in truly practical ways.

The ultimate state in life is to be free of attachment to labels, free of all the thoughts people have about where they are in terms of their progress. Instead we simply show up in every moment and each situation. We don't think in terms of future permanency, but rather create a meaningful life in each moment as it arises.

To be nonattached in this way means we no longer have to prove anything, no longer have to convince either ourselves or others of our worth. In my own case, in my attempt to prove my worth and the validity of my values and beliefs, I lost so much that I counted important—my initial wealth, my health, and my marriage. Yet through all of this, nothing of real value was ever lost. In fact life has an amazing way of even recycling some of the aspects of our experience in order to show us that nothing *can* ultimately be lost.

Earlier I spoke of how I had been forced to choose between my father and the daughter of his partner, which cost me a life with the woman I had intended to marry. Following this split in the partnership, my father and his partners were no longer on speaking terms. But when I was stricken with cancer, it served as an opportunity for them to speak again. Some showed up for my surgery, while others showed up when I went through chemotherapy.

One person asked me, "Was it worth all you went through to see everyone come back together?" My answer was in the affirmative, which engendered considerable surprise because it reveals just how important it is to continue caring for one another even when we experience a rupture in our relationships.

This approach enables us to embrace the authenticity that's continually seeking to arise within us and transform our experience of everyday reality. Perhaps you see it as surrendering to God, or maybe to a universal consciousness. It doesn't matter how we articulate it. In the end we embrace what each of us has the potential to be individually, along with what we have the potential to be *together*.

In a commencement speech at Stanford, Steve Jobs remarked that we can only connect the dots backwards. When we do so, we see how everything we have experienced is a steppingstone toward what is to come. So whatever you may be doing and whatever may be happening in your life, just be open. Know that you are where you are for a reason.

I think of how my father had been buying from Eastern Europe. In 1981 my family drove through some of the regions where he had done business since the 1970s. Not only were there ridiculous borders with barbed wire and machine guns, there were also snipers. Since we weren't supposed to have local money, we hid it in tennis rackets. Because you can't connect the dots ahead of time and therefore must seize opportunities as they present themselves, little could I have guessed that ten years later I would be operating in these countries and would do so for the next 20 years.

My major in university was entrepreneurship in family businesses, which of course connects to Qineticare, where I have the honor to serve closely knit family businesses and family offices. The loss of my health led to spending my life helping others avoid what happened to me.

Whereas for many years I wasn't present in my life and had to learn how to be so, today I help others to be present.

Whereas I wasn't making healthy choices, today I show others how to make healthy choices. Whereas I didn't have ways to detox emotionally, today I assist people in finding the right coaches and mentors so they can discover how to function at an optimal level. Whereas I ended up divorced, I now help many couples with their relationships. Even those who can't escape a split discover how to do it amicably, while those who stay together learn to be understanding of the masculine and the feminine, which helps them begin to love at a level they never thought possible.

In these and other ways, I look back and see how life has connected the dots. It's as if I've come full circle. Although life had to beat me over the head in three ways to get me to pay attention, I was fortunately at last able to listen, download, and execute.

The multinationals I represented loved me because I listened and executed. They didn't have to either babysit me or push me. They trusted me, and I them. It's only possible to give all you can give if you trust instead of constantly second-guessing the other person's motives. Second-guessing will zap your creativity and sap your energy.

Many have asked me over the years, "Why are you wasting your time with all of these guys from the multinationals? You're going to build their brands, then they're going to get rid of you." What such people don't realize is that the process of building a brand has value in and of itself. It's the experience that's the most valuable aspect. Why do I trust instead of second-guessing? My answer is, Why second-guess when you could be learning so much?

If I stopped to think about all the kicks I've been on the receiving end of, I would trust no one. I wouldn't participate. I would just conclude that this world is the most horrendous place in the cosmos, then get out my golf clubs. Instead I operate from the kind of openness and trust we've been discussing. I see everything as preparing me, developing me, bringing out aspects of my potential of which I have no awareness.

The truth is, I don't know how to live any other way. I do things because they are the *right* thing to do. Head and heart unite in an unconditional "Yes!" to every aspect of my life.

It doesn't matter whether I'm expending energy and others don't get what I'm seeking to convey, or whether they may not want to listen because they aren't aligned. It's not about whether a venture brings me a return, as long as I do what's authentic in any particular moment. What matters is that there's no second-guessing and no trying to connect the dots in the future, just confidence in life's flow. With this approach, I find that I sleep peacefully, arise each morning enthusiastically, and go through my day lovingly...and now with a beloved and loving partner beyond all expectation.

I much prefer this way of living to the unbalanced lifestyle that brought me to my knees through cancer.

How about you? Do you know of any better way to live?

REFLECTIONS:

Four Steps to Flow

The key to a meaningful life is to embrace changes and challenges in a calm, relaxed manner—something that's possible only to the degree we are in tune with our essential being. From here, we move forward in trust, entering into a state of inner calm, which results in clarity and leads to a life lived in flow.

Four steps take us into the stream of flow.

STEP ONE: EMBRACE

When a business investment fails, a serious health issue arises, or someone significant exits our life for one reason or another, our reaction is all but predictable. We tend to recoil and resist.

The last thing we're likely to conclude at such a time is that what's happening is for our benefit. Although it may not look like it, any disruptive change is an invitation to convert the challenge we are faced with into an opportunity.

Pause for a moment to think back to a time when a severe

reversal plunged your life into turmoil. What was the nature of the crisis? What challenges were you faced with? What were the feelings that arose within you?

After perhaps an initial shock, did you experience sadness, despair, a sense of helplessness...and maybe even hopelessness?

Now let's think beyond this state. Wasn't there a point at which you glimpsed a way forward? In that moment, you identified an opportunity.

When you did so, the nature of the challenge you were dealing with was transformed. What looked like at least a setback, if not a disaster, became the opening to new vistas and fresh horizons.

What happened is that you dissolved your resistance by embracing the change that was occurring in your life. A potential setback became a springboard.

What change in your life at this moment is calling for you to release your resistance and embrace the change? And if you do, what opportunities would present themselves?

To embrace a situation is fundamentally different from what most of us mean when we speak of "surrender." When I hear people speak of surrender, they almost always think we are supposed to surrender to our situation. It doesn't seem to occur to them that what life might really be asking of us is to open up to something within ourselves that's seeking to be recognized and embraced.

What it takes to live in flow is authenticity, which is to live from our essential being. This is the aspect of us that's always real. It's impossible to be in flow when we aren't being genuine. When we are authentic, we don't worry about how we might come across. It doesn't concern us whether we are matching up to people's expectations. We don't even worry whether we are living up to our potential. We recognize that only ego concerns itself with such matters. The real person is content to just be the individual we spontaneously find ourselves to be in each moment. As we quit "advertising" ourselves, which is the ego's blimpish way of going about things, we instead embark on simply being real. This is what we are asked to embrace about ourselves.

What change or crisis has presented you with an opportunity to invite a more authentic way of being in every facet of your everyday life? In what ways did this change allow you to move beyond the defensiveness of your ego? Can you identify aspects of your originally peaceful, joyous, loving self that have been able to break through as a result of this change?

STEP TWO: TRUST

When we embrace change instead of pushing back, something magical happens. We find ourselves moving into a state of trust, whereby we spontaneously move forward confidently.

We have an innate ability to have any tendency to get upset over an issue shift into trust. Observe how two children who fall out over a toy in the sandpit are soon playing happily together again. To trust is a natural trait that comes with being human.

four steps to flow

Can you think of a time when you at first became upset with someone or with a situation, only to experience a renewed sense of trust as the issue was resolved? What did it feel like to have your anxiety, anger, or disappointment subside?

No matter our age, at any moment we can awaken afresh to the realization that many occurrences that initially appear threatening are actually the universe beckoning us to adventure. Once we recognize this, we are ready to trust our ability to seize the opportunity that is presenting itself.

Trust in our ability to begin again needs to come from far deeper than positive thinking, which can only carry us so far. It needs to be rooted in who we are in our essential being, our authentic self. These are the kinds of tools the ego relies on.

Have you realized yet that you can't talk yourself into an enduring state of trust? Self-talk at best produces a pseudo self-confidence that when tested collapses. Abiding trust isn't about hyping ourselves up. It involves a much deeper sense that we are up for whatever life sends our way—joyously so.

Change invites an authentic, trusting way of being to erupt into every facet of our everyday life. At such times, our originally peaceful, joyous, loving self is seeking to break through our belief that we aren't good enough and need to somehow prove ourselves.

When we move beyond a need to prove ourselves to others—or even to ourselves—our expectations of what's possible for our lives undergo a considerable upscaling, as a result of which we no longer tolerate mediocrity. To accept the me-

214

diocre is the opposite of trust.

Pause to reflect on a time when you failed to fully embrace life—to believe in its goodness and your our own potential to stretch yourself to accomplish beyond your imagination. Why were you willing to tolerate mediocrity? What was behind your low level of faith in life and in yourself?

How sad that so many tolerate rather than celebrate life. Trust is about first embracing, then entrusting ourselves to, whatever may be unfolding.

STEP THREE: CALMNESS

If we are to make wise choices at critical moments, we require clarity. Such clarity emerges from embracing whatever may be occurring, approaching life in a trusting manner, and engaging challenges from a calm inner centeredness. It's when our thoughts are quiet instead of running wild, and our emotions calm instead of in turmoil, that clarity can emerge.

It has become common to pit heart against head. You hear people say, "Get out of your mind and into your heart." This comes from a failure to understand the difference between our intelligence and the mental chatter we experience. When we go deep enough, we discover within ourselves the sound of sheer silence. This silence speaks the language of realness, which always makes logical sense.

This realness is quite distinct from our jumbled and often confusing thoughts and emotions. It's utterly different in character from all the voices in our head that constantly clamor for our attention, let alone the passions that seize us and cause us to make irrational, emotionally-driven choices.

It's important to be aware that feelings can generate emotion, but we should be careful not to confuse emotion with the deeper currents of our heart. We all experience occasions when our emotions are diametrically opposite to what we truly feel at the core of our being.

When change is forced on us, instead of scrambling to know what to do next, the stillness that arises within us when we choose to embrace the change allows us to hear ourselves think in a way we haven't until now. We also find ourselves aware of what we truly feel about things, which may be quite different from what we've been told all our life we're supposed to feel.

Can you think of a time when quieting your racing thoughts, coupled with emotional calmness, allowed the kind of insight to emerge that served to unite the wisdom of both your head and your heart? As head and heart came together, in what ways did you find yourself moving from chaos to clarity?

It's to quiet their thoughts and thereby allow clarity to arise that even major corporations are encouraging their personnel to spend a little time in meditation. Let me be clear that when I use the word "meditation," I'm not referring to a particular form of meditation, but to simply sitting in stillness in a manner that opens up the heart and mind so that we become truly aware. Sitting in stillness is a gateway to our inner self, allowing us to tap into the infinite pool of wisdom within. Establishing a consistent practice of sitting in stillness enables us to approach life with imagination and enthusiasm.

STEP FOUR: CLARITY

The clarity we require if we are to make wise choices at critical moments arises when head and heart come together. When we are in our head alone, or our heart alone, flow simply isn't possible. Instead we are likely to experience a pseudo form of flow, the kind of walking on air feeling two people may experience when they "fall in love" and engage in a fling that causes them to leave their marriages, often with disastrous results.

The ability to keep a cool head no matter what brings us to the step that empowers us to turn challenge into opportunity. When we know something is the right thing, we believe in it. We trust the direction we are taking. The determination and the wisdom we require to achieve the result we seek arise spontaneously from within.

Using our intelligence and our feelings enables us to embrace whatever may be unfolding in our lives. Because we bring the whole of ourselves to our challenges, we are keenly aware of all the factors in a situation. Not easily blindsided, we make smart decisions. Instead of scrambling to know what to do next, our calm but fully engaged state allows us to feel and hear ourselves think in a way we haven't until now. Since we are attuned to the profound inner stillness of our center, we intuitively "sense" whatever we need to know.

The insight that comes to us makes it possible for us to invest ourselves in pursuing a way forward with intentionality. Consequently we shift from chaos to clarity.

Ponder a challenging time in your life. In what ways is what you feel about it perhaps different from what you were told all your life you are "supposed" to feel or ought to feel?

As you think back to a particular situation, dwell for a few moments on the ways in which the quieting of your racing thoughts, along with a growing emotional calmness, allowed the kind of insight to emerge that unites the wisdom of both head and heart?

RESULT: A LIFE LIVED IN FLOW

When people think of flow, they tend to associate it with being in the "zone," which is a sense of being outside of time that athletes in particular seem able to enter into briefly during competition. This is however only a window into what flow is all about. Would you believe that the whole of your life can unfold in a state of flow?

Not only is this possible, but it's our most natural mode of being—so much so that it's one of the most compelling reasons I sit in stillness for a period each day. The effects of this simple practice are akin to taking time off for a vacation. Little by little we find ourselves becoming calm, peaceful, and above all receptive—and then life begins to come together.

The synergy of mental clarity and deep feeling that arises in this state enables us to bring flow to every aspect of our day. Whatever we may be doing, head and heart unite in dynamic action that's free of all pressure and therefore requires no drivenness in order for us to achieve our goals.

Picture flow as a centered life in which there's complete

balance. To either side of this centered state lies one of two unbalanced modes of making our way in the world. One of these modes involves needing to prove ourselves. When we operate in this mode, we are in a state of resistance to whatever may be happening. The other mode is one in which we tend to capitulate to our circumstances.

Think about your life as you are experiencing it at the present moment. To which of these two unbalanced modes do you find yourself tending? Are you inclined to be driven, as I was? Or do you allow life to toss you around as you tell yourself something is or isn't "meant to be," as if fate were orchestrating your life?

The question that tends to haunt us all is, Am I good enough? It's our inability to feel that we are enough that causes us to veer away from the kind of balance that promotes flow. Trying to be "good enough" involves wearing a mask and putting on an act, both of which soon become tiring. The relaxed state we refer to as flow is the result of living authentically. We can only flow when we are being real, which is a matter of being true to ourselves.

Consider the behavior you engage in. Can you identify some aspect of your life in which you find it a challenge to be real? Bring to mind the feeling of falseness you experience as you go about your activities in a way that isn't entirely genuine. How might you shift into authenticity in this dimension of your life? What changes might you make were your head and heart to become united, so that your whole being comes together in a powerful "Yes" to who you would truly like to be?

When change is forced upon us, we have an opportunity to step out of our drivenness on the one hand and any sense of being a victim of our circumstances on the other. We can free ourselves from the need to prove ourselves and any tendency to capitulate to the pressures we may be experiencing.

Change, especially when it involves crisis, clears the way for us to have our whole life unfold from the flow that accompanies being truly present in whatever we are doing—whether our work, an evening of romance, or a simple task such as washing the dishes.

To live in flow is to move beyond the ego's need to rate one thing as more important than another, causing us to rush through certain activities in order to get to the next. Flow means that whatever may be occurring in this moment is important. If it's on our front burner, it deserves our full attention.

It isn't enough to experience flow only in short bursts. It's possible to have each and every decision come from that place deep within us where intelligence and feeling no longer clash, but function synergistically to bring us the maximum fulfillment life is able to provide.

When we have nothing to prove, we exude a trust and confidence that are grounded in the stillness of our deep center. This allows us to get clear in our own mind what we need to do, which we then accomplish as an expression of flow. We don't worry about how we might come across. It doesn't concern us whether we are matching up to other people's expectations. We don't even worry whether we are living up to our potential. We recognize that only ego concerns itself with such matters. The real person each of us is finds itself content to just be the person we are.

The state of flow is one in which we are able to be truly present with other people. Our presence flows from the fact we are at last really present with ourselves—awake, aware, and therefore attentive and focused. This is because we are no longer battling energy-sucking issues such as a lack of self-acceptance and self-confidence. Because we now embrace ourselves in every way, we fully embrace every dimension of our lives.

In our highly conscious state, we sweep nothing under the carpet, instead dealing with issues as they arise. Consequently we are in integrity with ourselves and with others. In each and every situation, we are aligned with our values and do the thing that's right.

When people are in flow, no longer motivated by a need to prove themselves or by comparing themselves to others, we will create a world in which we care for one another, contributing our insights, gifts, and creativity for the benefit of everyone.

About the Author

Feisal Alibhai, a serial entrepreneur who has lived on five continents and founded more than a dozen companies, is today the founder and CEO of Qineticare, the world's first Family Health Office. Based between Hong Kong and Switzerland, he shares a revolutionary approach to health, wellbeing, and the art of living in flow with multigenerational families across the globe.

At the peak of his entrepreneurial success beginning in his 30s, while employing more than 10,000 people, he was faced with three life-changing crises. Coming within an inch of his life, he recognized that he needed to immerse himself in a multidimensional approach to life. These experiences taught him that, irrespective of one's education or wealth, unexpected financial, health, and relationship challenges are rarely handled well.

Born in the Democratic Republic of Congo and of Indian descent, he was raised in Belgium, finished his schooling in Canada, and graduated from The Wharton School, University of Pennsylvania. He today enjoys a state of wellbeing beyond anything he experienced before the three crises struck, pioneering a quality of life we all deserve.